ARENDT: A GUIDE FOR THE PERPLEXED

Continuum *Guides for the Perplexed*

Continuum's Guides for the Perplexed are clear, concise and accessible introductions to thinkers, writers and subjects that students and readers can find especially challenging. Concentrating specifically on what it is that makes the subject difficult to grasp, these books explain and explore key themes and ideas, guiding the reader towards a thorough understanding of demanding material.

***Guides for the Perplexed* available from Continuum**

Adorno: A Guide for the Perplexed, Alex Thomson
Arendt: A Guide for the Perplexed, Karin Fry
Aristotle: A Guide for the Perplexed, John Vella
Berkeley: A Guide for the Perplexed, Talia Bettcher
Deleuze: A Guide for the Perplexed, Claire Colebrook
Derrida: A Guide for the Perplexed, Julian Wolfreys
Descartes: A Guide for the Perplexed, Justin Skirry
Existentialism: A Guide for the Perplexed, Stephen Earnshaw
Freud: A Guide for the Perplexed, Celine Surprenant
Gadamer: A Guide for the Perplexed, Chris Lawn
Habermas: A Guide for the Perplexed, Eduardo Mendieta
Hegel: A Guide for the Perplexed, David James
Heidegger: A Guide for the Perplexed, David Cerbone
Hobbes: A Guide for the Perplexed, Stephen J. Finn
Hume: A Guide for the Perplexed, Angela Coventry
Husserl: A Guide for the Perplexed, Matheson Russell
Kant: A Guide for the Perplexed, T. K. Seung
Kierkegaard: A Guide for the Perplexed, Clare Carlisle
Leibniz: A Guide for the Perplexed, Franklin Perkins
Levinas: A Guide for the Perplexed, B. C. Hutchens
Merleau-Ponty: A Guide for the Perplexed, Eric Matthews
Nietzsche: A Guide for the Perplexed, R. Kevin Hill
Plato: A Guide for the Perplexed, Gerald A. Press
Pragmatism: A Guide for the Perplexed, Robert B. Talisse and Scott F. Aikin
Quine: A Guide for the Perplexed, Gary Kemp
Relativism: A Guide for the Perplexed, Timothy Mosteller
Ricoeur: A Guide for the Perplexed, David Pellauer
Rousseau: A Guide for the Perplexed, Matthew Simpson
Sartre: A Guide for the Perplexed, Gary Cox
Spinoza: A Guide for the Perplexed, Charles Jarrett
The Stoics: A Guide for the Perplexed, M. Andrew Holowchak
Wittgenstein: A Guide for the Perplexed, Mark Addis

ARENDT: A GUIDE FOR THE PERPLEXED

KARIN FRY

Continuum International Publishing Group

The Tower Building
11 York Road
London SE1 7NX

80 Maiden Lane
Suite 704
New York NY 10038

www.continuumbooks.com

British Library Cataloguing-in-Publication Data
A catalogue record for this book is available from the British Library.

ISBN: HB: 0-8264-9985-6
PB: 0-8264-9986-4
HB: 978-0-8264-9985-1
PB: 978-0-8264-9986-8

Library of Congress Cataloging-in-Publication Data
Fry, Karin A.
Arendt : a guide for the perplexed / Karin A. Fry.
p. cm.
ISBN 978-0-8264-9985-1 – ISBN 978-0-8264-9986-8
1. Arendt, Hannah, 1906–1975. I. Title.

JC251.A74F79 2008
320.5–dc22

2008037000

Typeset by Newgen Imaging Systems Pvt Ltd, Chennai, India
Printed and bound in Great Britain by MPG Books Ltd, Bodmin, Cornwall

To William
and to Rogue for taking care of him

CONTENTS

ABBREVIATIONS

WORKS BY HANNAH ARENDT

BF	*Between Friends: The Correspondence of Hannah Arendt and Mary McCarthy, 1949–1975*
BPF	*Between Past and Future*
CR	*Crises of the Republic*
EJ	*Eichmann in Jerusalem*
EU	*Essays in Understanding*
HC	*The Human Condition*
JC	*Hannah Arendt Karl Jaspers Correspondence, 1926–1969*
KPP	*Lectures on Kant's Political Philosophy*
LM	*Life of the Mind*
MDT	*Men in Dark Times*
OR	*On Revolution*
OT	*The Origins of Totalitarianism*
PA	*The Portable Arendt*
PP	*The Promise of Politics*
RJ	*Responsibility and Judgment*
RLC	*Reflections on Literature and Culture*
RV	*Rahel Varnhagen: The Life of a Jewish Woman*
WFW	*Within Four Walls: The Correspondence between Hannah Arendt and Heinrich Blücher, 1936–1968*

INTRODUCTION

Hannah Arendt is an important and controversial political thinker whose views are not easily labelled. Unlike many of the other famous philosophers of her day who used a great deal of philosophical jargon, Arendt is a clear writer who often wrote for the general public, not merely academic audiences, making many of her ideas somewhat assessable for the newcomer to her thought. However, Arendt was also an extremely prolific writer who examined many topics, making it almost impossible for one to understand an overview of her thought quickly. This book will explain the many different facets of Arendt's theory in order to show how her theory fits together as a whole. Arendt rarely changed her theoretical positions throughout her career and each book that she added to her corpus explored an additional aspect that expanded upon the rest of her theory. In general, Arendt's work can be understood as an answer to what she thought was the most important problem of her time: totalitarianism. Though her writing builds upon itself, Arendt's work cannot be thought of as a rigid, inflexible system. The entirety of Arendt's theory supports the importance of different viewpoints and tries to avoid the smothering of the free exchange of ideas that is commonplace in totalitarian governments. Arendt's theory does not seek to pin down all experience into a rigid theoretical map, but strives to understand the multifaceted nature of political life by emphasizing the importance of new and different perspectives coming into the world. This means that the reader must approach Arendt's work as a framework for understanding politics that begins a conversation, rather than making conclusive claims that suppress any dissention.

Hannah Arendt was born Johanna Cohn Arendt in Hanover, Germany in 1906 to a middle-class secular Jewish family and spent her childhood in Königsberg, East Prussia, now Kalingrad, Russia. Königsberg was associated with philosophy since it was the town in which the famous philosopher Immanuel Kant lived, worked and studied in the late eighteenth and early nineteenth centuries. After her father died when she was 7, Arendt and her mother moved to Berlin. As a young woman, Arendt became interested in philosophy and by the age of 14, knew that she would study it. Her passion for philosophy was so intense and her need to understand so great, that she claimed that she would have to study philosophy or drown herself, so to speak (*PA* 9). Her earliest interests included Immanuel Kant's philosophy and the existential theory of Karl Jaspers and Soren Kierkegaard (*PA* 9). She attended university in Marburg, Germany from 1924–1926, where she was introduced to Martin Heidegger's philosophy during the time when he was writing his famous book *Being and Time.* Heidegger's abstract philosophy and charismatic personality drew students to Marburg and when Arendt was 18, she began a secret love affair with Heidegger who was married and had two children. The constraints of Heidegger's marriage and family made the affair difficult, and Arendt moved to pursue an advanced degree in philosophy in Heidelberg, Germany with Karl Jaspers. According to Arendt, Jaspers was the most significant influence on her intellectual development. Jaspers' philosophy was more concrete than Heidegger's theory, and Jaspers had a greater emphasis on communication and politics, rather exclusively focusing on metaphysical truths. Arendt was also attracted to Jasper's concept of freedom that linked action to reason (*PA* 21). During the Second World War, she lost touch with Jaspers for seven years and feared for his safety. Jaspers' wife, Gertrud, was Jewish and Jaspers was barred from teaching and publishing during the war by the National Socialist government. Once Arendt and Jaspers realized that they had survived the war, they began a close professional and personal friendship that was extremely important to both of them. The friendship lasted until Jaspers' death in 1969.[1]

Arendt stated that she was not interested in politics when she was young and her first theoretical interests were situated firmly within the tradition of German philosophy (*PA* 392). For her dissertation, she wrote on the concept of love in St Augustine and published it in 1929, the same year that she applied for a stipend to study German Romanticism. Later, in a letter to Karl Jaspers, Arendt admitted that she initially was politically naïve and found the 'so-called Jewish question boring' (*JC* 197). In fact, the word 'Jew' was rarely mentioned in her home, and she claimed that she did not know from her family that she was Jewish, though she was not surprised when she heard antisemitic remarks on the street from other children (*PA* 7–8). Her family were not practicing Jews, but were also not ashamed of their ethnicity, and handled antisemitic behaviour by defending themselves as Jews, refusing to feel inferior, and not letting it get to them (*PA* 90). Arendt did not practice the religion of Judaism, though she did request that her husband, Heinrich Blücher, have a Jewish funeral when he died, even though he was not Jewish (*JC* 166).[2]

If the world had not changed, one wonders what topics Arendt would have explored throughout her life. But it was the political climate in which she lived that changed the focus of her primary intellectual concerns. For Arendt, a decisive event for her life was the burning of the Reichstag and the following arrests of that night in 1933. At that point, she began to feel responsible for the political situation and could no longer claim to be a bystander (*PA* 6). She saw the rise of Nazi Germany first hand, lost many friends and was forced to emigrate from her home. In fact, Martin Heidegger's involvement with National Socialism deeply disturbed her, and she lost contact with him for 17 years. In 1933, she became involved with the Zionist movement, using her academic background as a justifiable cover for library research in the Prussian State Library that aimed at recording the antisemitic acts of private groups in Germany. After several weeks of research, she was arrested and the police had difficulty reading one of her coded notebooks that was in a familiar philosophical language: Greek.[3] She was released after eight days, largely because she befriended her captor and made up stories to tell him about her activities. Once released, she immediately left Berlin with her mother, unwilling to take the chance of being arrested again. She crossed illegally through the forest into Czechoslovakia and began 18 years of being a stateless person. She settled in Paris for many years and worked for Youth Aliyah, which helped move Jewish children to Palestine, until the rise of the Vichy government forced her into a French internment camp in Gurs, France in 1940. Her escape from the camp included a great measure of luck. During the confusion when the Germans invaded France, Arendt left the camp though she was told to stay by the French officials and wait for the Germans to occupy the camp. After her escape, she eventually immigrated to New York with her second husband, Heinrich Blücher, and her mother, who soon followed thereafter. Arendt later discovered that those who stayed in the camp were sent on trains to Auschwitz.[4]

Arendt lived the rest of her life in the United States and became a citizen in 1951, ten years after entering the country. Arendt arrived without knowing any English, but learned the language quickly and eventually published primarily in English.[5] Her early career involved various writing, editing and translating projects, as well as working for Jewish organizations. As her books attained public recognition, she became more involved in the academic community, gave public lectures and eventually taught seminars in political theory at several universities, including Princeton, the University of California, Berkeley, The University of Chicago, and ended her career with a full-time post at The New School for Social Research in New York City.

Arendt believed that thinking was inspired by personal experience (*PA* 19). The experiences of her life led her to a deep understanding of the importance of politics and her academic interests were devoted to understanding the relationship between philosophical theory and political practice. Arendt maintained that the Jewish question was the focal point of her intellectual work and credited her husband, Heinrich Blücher, with helping her to 'think politically and see historically' (*JC* 31). Wanting to understand how even brilliant intellectuals, like Martin Heidegger, could misunderstand the political horror of the Nazi regime prompted book projects, many of which examined the relationship between intellectual theory and politics. It was not the behaviour of the enemy that surprised Arendt, but the betrayals of her friends in the intellectual community that inspired such an anti-academic mood in her that it made her want to reject academia altogether (*PA* 11). Arendt claimed that she was shocked by how easily most of the German intelligentsia became friends with the Nazi regime and how many of them became fellow criminals (*JW* 493). Overall, she left Europe with a deep suspicion of philosophy, intellectuals and academic life. Even though her graduate work was in philosophy, she would later state in an interview:

> [I]n my opinion I have said good-bye to philosophy once and for all. As you know I studied philosophy, but that does not mean I stayed with it . . . I want to look at politics so to speak with eyes unclouded by philosophy. (*PA* 3–4)

The irony of this move is notable, since most of Hannah Arendt's writing concerned the discussion of major figures in the history of Western philosophy, but she thought that there was a tension between philosophy and politics and that the intellectual activity of abstract thinking led philosophers to dismiss political action as less significant than contemplation.[6] She believed that the profession of being an intellectual could sometimes inspire political folly because it concerned fabricating ideas that allowed certain thinkers to make up interesting things to say about everything, even Nazism, which Arendt found to be 'grotesque' (*PA* 12). Her departure from Germany was also a departure from academia, and she was motivated to do practical social work in France. From 1933–1944, Arendt wrote mainly journalistic pieces as opposed to academic ones, and throughout the rest of her career, she denied the title of philosopher and preferred to be called a political theorist (*PA* 4, *EU* xxv).

In spite of her disavowal of philosophy, Hannah Arendt's method of doing theory was grounded in philosophy and influenced by many philosophical figures. Arendt never fully discussed her method, but she claimed that she was a 'kind of' phenomenologist, but one that differed from G. W. F. Hegel or Edmund Husserl.[7] Phenomenology is a type of philosophy that begins with the lived experience of the human being, which was the starting point for Arendt's thought, but she did not build an all encompassing systematic philosophy like Hegel and Husserl. Arendt's intellectual interests usually concerned human political phenomena, rather than ontological or metaphysical questions about the nature of the universe. The philosophies of Immanuel Kant and Karl Jaspers were important to Arendt, because both emphasized practical and political issues.[8] Arendt often referenced practical political philosophers like Cicero, Montesquieu, Jefferson and Adams in her work. Socrates was a significant influence, since he promoted a sense of intellectual interrogation of the self that Arendt thought was the key to thinking and morality, and Augustine inspired her view of the importance of natality, or the aspect of humanity that can begin and initiate new acts in the world. Nietzsche and Heidegger were also important because Arendt began most essays with an examination of language and the origins of various political concepts, in order to trace how ideas had changed throughout time. Most of her work employed a method that traced the topic of discussion back to its original meaning to see how its meaning had changed and whether there had been intellectual confusion concerning it that had amassed over the centuries. Finally, perhaps Arendt's greatest influence was Aristotle because following Aristotle, she sought to clarify different categories in order to combat intellectual confusion. She stated that she began any topic by distinguishing between A and B, and she traced this method to Aristotle. She asserted that her chief frustration with contemporary history and political science was their 'growing incapacity for making distinctions', and that political terms were becoming so general that they were losing all meaning (*PA* 162). Much of her work involved investigating the history of various terms and defining them in distinctive ways.

Arendt's description of Walter Benjamin's method is revealing, since she referenced it on occasion when she described her own work.[9] Arendt claimed that Benjamin was like a pearl diver who excavated the depths of history to pry loose and bring the surface rich and strange pearls and corals from the depths. These pearls and corals were thought fragments that were brought to the surface, not to reinstitute their past life or significance, but to show how there had been a crystallization of past thought that had changed by years in the sea, but could be illuminating to us (*MDT* 205–6). In *The Life of the Mind*, Arendt described her own method similarly by talking about the strange pearls and coral thought fragments that she wrestled from the fragmented tradition and examined after their sea change in history (*LM* I, 212). Margaret Canovan, a prominent Arendt scholar, describes Arendt's use of the past as having two tasks. First, Arendt sought to articulate theory that more accurately represented the phenomena that it sought to describe by making productive distinctions between concepts and second, Arendt desired to make use of past possibilities that were described theoretically, but never realized.[10] Arendt's examination of the past was not a nostalgic longing to bring back past types of living, nor an investigation of factual events, but a fruitful dive that was meant to find theoretical treasures that could be useful to us and could clarify present types of political phenomena. Arendt was fond of the William Faulkner quote 'the past is never dead, it's not even past' (*RJ* 270). Similarly, her dives into the past were meant to have political significance for the present and for the future.

This book will examine Arendt's political philosophy, both by describing the view of politics and philosophy that she was against, as well as explaining the positive features of her thought. It is organized roughly historically, covering main themes in her work, without suggesting that her theory can be catalogued into different phases or periods, since she tended to revisit topics repeatedly over time. The first chapter examines the type of politics that Arendt was always theorizing against: totalitarianism. Chapter one discusses how totalitarianism emerged politically and what political and individual failures caused it to happen. Chapter two examines Arendt's positive political philosophy that prioritized political action and promoted the thriving of differences between persons. Chapter three covers further additions to her political theory, including her discussion of freedom and the importance of tradition, as well as her take on the practical political controversies of her day. The fourth chapter concerns her last work on the mental faculties of thinking, willing and political judgment. Finally, the last chapter summarizes Arendt's various critics. Arendt remains a very controversial figure and this chapter discusses the most important criticisms made against her theory, as well as her possible responses to some of these worries. Overall, I will argue that Arendt's work can be understood as a reaction to the rise of totalitarian politics and the inadequacy of traditional philosophical political theory in handling the diverse views of the people that are necessary for democratic politics. Arendt believed that traditional philosophical theory that frames politics universally has tyrannical tendencies and the uniting theme throughout her work is to rethink these political categories to encourage a more democratic politics that supports pluralism and differences between persons.

Interestingly, despite Arendt's tensions with philosophy and its neglect of politics, Arendt did not think of herself as a political actor, but as a thinker. Arendt described her own work as an effort to try to understand what is happening.[11] It was the thought process of struggling with a problem that was important to her and writing motivated her to engage in that struggle. In fact, she attributed whatever success she had in understanding politics to the fact that she looked at politics from the outside, from the perspective of a thinker.[12] As an outsider to both politics and traditional philosophy, Arendt maintained an unpredictable and unique perspective, which spurred a great deal of controversy concerning her ideas. Though this book may implicitly defend some of Arendt's views, it seeks mainly to clarify her thought in her own terms, rather than to defend it. Arendt claimed that 'everything I did and everything I wrote – all that is tentative. I think that all thinking, the way that I have indulged in it perhaps a little beyond measure, extravagantly, has the earmark of being tentative.'[13] Hannah Arendt began a conversation and it is up to us to continue it.

CHAPTER ONE

TOTALITARIANISM AND THE BANALITY OF EVIL

In her most famous work, *The Human Condition*, Hannah Arendt claims that her intellectual project concerns 'nothing more than to think what we are doing' (*HC* 5). This phrase captures the spirit of Arendt's work, which concerns understanding theory and its relationship to everyday political practices in the world. Shaped by her own experiences during the war, it is natural that Arendt would want to understand what happened and why, in an effort to avoid replicating such horror. One of her earliest works, *The Origins of Totalitarianism* (1951), and a work that she wrote mid-career, *Eichmann in Jerusalem* (1963), attempt to explain the rise of totalitarian regimes in the twentieth century and examine the conditions that allowed for such brutality to occur. In *The Origins of Totalitarianism*, Arendt puts forward one of the first theories of totalitarianism that ambitiously seeks to explain totalitarianism in Nazi Germany and Stalinist Russia by tracing the history of race-thinking and imperialism that led to such movements. *Eichmann in Jerusalem*, written several years after *The Origins of Totalitarianism*, is an account of Adolf Eichmann's trial in Jerusalem for crimes against the Jewish people, crimes against humanity and war crimes. By attending the trial and hearing testimony, Arendt seeks to understand how Eichmann involved himself in such cruelty without remorse. Witnessing Eichmann's testimony prompts Arendt to theorize about the mechanisms within the individual person that allow totalitarianism to flourish. Taken together, the books explain the phenomena of totalitarianism at the level of both the state and the individual. They represent Arendt's criticisms of totalitarian political thought, and her positive political theory, which will be described in the following chapters, is best understood as an attempt to counter this form of politics.

The Origins of Totalitarianism is the book that established Arendt as an international scholar and the first book that she wrote in English, instead of her native German. In her preface to part one, Hannah Arendt states that the book is 'an attempt at understanding what at first and even second glance appeared simply outrageous' (*OT* xiv). What Arendt is primarily referring to is the Holocaust, a state-sanctioned operation of death that resulted in the murder of more than 6 million people, primarily Jews. Arendt begins writing *The Origins of Totalitarianism* 1945 and 1946, right at the end of the war and in direct response to the political climate of her day. Arendt believes that the questions concerning the emergence of the totalitarianism were the most urgent questions of her generation and that it was necessary to explain what happened and why in order to avoid such atrocities in the future. Published in 1951, the book initially received some enthusiastically positive reviews, but was also criticized for a variety of reasons, largely having to do with the uneven treatment between Nazism and Stalinism, since Nazism is covered much more extensively than Stalinism. However, despite the criticisms made against it, Arendt's work remains one of the first important attempts to make sense of the senselessness of totalitarianism, in which politics turns against itself and no longer concerns the common good of the people, but strives for long-term ideological goals resulting in the death and destruction of significant portions of the population.

The Origins of Totalitarianism is a book that is hard to classify, not strictly history, sociology or philosophy and it mainly focuses on giving a historical account to the multifaceted factors that allowed for totalitarian thinking to dominate in Europe in the early to middle twentieth century. Arendt was never satisfied with the book, or with the title, and it is clear that some further editing would make it a stronger book. However, Arendt let the book go to press, despite her dissatisfaction, because she thought that the problems it addressed were urgent and needed to be examined publicly as soon as possible.[1] Answering one of her critics, Eric Voegelin, Arendt explains that her frustration with the book concerned the fact that it was an attempt at both a historical account and a negative critique and attack, aimed at the destruction of totalitarianism (*PA* 158). This differs from most historical writing, because it is not a positive attempt to account for and preserve the history of a culture, but a negative attack to discuss what went wrong historically. In this way, the book is more of a genealogy of modes of thought, than a history of facts.

The typical philosophical approach to the problem of totalitarianism would be to try to define the essence of the political system of totalitarianism, but Arendt does not describe an essence to totalitarianism, because she thinks it is a new phenomenon that emerges in human history and does not have some kind of eternal, essential features. Arendt's view of totalitarianism also differs from the more common accounts that stress the frozen, rigid and planned nature of the National Socialist movement. As Margaret Canovan notes, Arendt's description of totalitarianism is that it is more like a hurricane levelling everything in its path, which is not deliberately planned or structured, but 'chaotic, non-utilitarian, manically dynamic movement of destruction that assails all the features of human nature and human world that might make politics possible'.[2] The first two sections of the book, titled 'Antisemitism' and 'Imperialism', examine historical and sociological factors that laid the groundwork for the hurricane of totalitarian thought that swept through Germany and Russia.[3]

ANTISEMITISM AND IMPERIALISM

'Antisemitism' and 'Imperialism' describe the factors that crystallized in the flourishing of a racist attitude in Europe in the early twentieth century, and in general, these sections trace the development of Nazism much more extensively than Stalinism. Though her title proclaims to concern the 'origins' of totalitarianism, Arendt asserts that she is not seeking to describe direct causation for totalitarianism, which according to Margaret Canovan, would be impossible since Arendt believes that human actions are free and a discussion of causal factors gives the impression that totalitarianism was unavoidable.[4] Rather, Arendt is trying to trace the history of elements that make the emergence of the new political formation of totalitarianism possible.

Arendt begins with a discussion of the development of the widespread belief in antisemitism in Europe. Arendt disagrees with some more common theories of her day concerning the treatment of Jews in Europe. She did not agree with the 'scapegoat' theory that proposes the need for an arbitrary group to be blamed for society's problems, because she thinks that it presumes that the scapegoat could have been another people (*OT* 5). For Arendt, the racism of Nazism is crucially linked to the Jews specifically and the main focus of the National Socialist political philosophy assumes a hatred and suspicion of the Jews that could not be easily replaced with another oppressed group. Arendt also does not believe in the theory that the Jews are an eternally oppressed people, because she argues that this position allows the Jews to avoid responsibility for their condition and encourages complacency in correcting the problem. In *The Origins of Totalitarianism*, Arendt controversially recounts certain historical aspects in which the Jews themselves are implicated. This does not mean that the Jews were responsible for the Holocaust, but merely that the common Jewish strategy for coping with racist oppression in Europe did not help them avoid it. It is Arendt's view that the Jews had a strange and special status in Europe and were never wholly assimilated. Their big mistake was that they did not seek full political rights. Often, Jews were favoured by various aristocratic courts because they offered the monarchy and aristocracy loans and wealth. This granted them certain political privileges and favours, but at the same time, they were still treated like a separate group without full political rights. By not thinking in terms of equal rights and accepting special favours and privileges, the Jews did not secure a more stable political future according to Arendt (*OT* 18). This problem was accentuated with the rise of the nation-state and the downfall of the monarchies, because the material value of the Jews to the state no longer existed. Since political rights were not secured, there was no incentive for the state to watch out for the welfare of the Jews, allowing the possibility of nationwide antisemitism to occur, which was a crucial step that led to the acceptance of Nazi ideology. As a stateless person herself when she was writing the book, Arendt makes the important point that human rights like the ones that Thomas Paine articulates in the 'Rights of Man' are only enforceable for persons who belong to a nation-state. Human rights, despite their claim to universality, become non-existent without citizenship and this factor continues to allow many persons throughout the world to have their basic human rights ignored. Arendt discusses this conundrum as the 'right to have rights' which is denied to persons without a nation (*OT* 296). Unfortunately, citizenship is the key to securing the right to political engagement and the European Jews, as a stateless people, were precariously at risk during the rise of totalitarianism because they did not have them.

Both in *The Origins of Totalitarianism* and in her earlier biography of the Jewish intellectual Rahel Varnhagen, Arendt focuses on what was called, 'the Jewish Question'. *Rahel Varnhagen: The Life of a Jewish Woman* (1957) is Arendt's first major work after her dissertation on St Augustine and it was largely written by 1933, except for the last two chapters that were written later (*RV* xiii).[5] The book examines the life of the salon hostess and Jewess, Rahel Varnhagen, and comments on the status of the Jews within Europe during the nineteenth century, especially the Jewish desire for acceptance and assimilation. Rahel Varnhagen was a Jewish society woman who eventually married a German nobleman and ultimately converted to Christianity. In her youth, Varnhagen's salon drew the most famous intellectuals and artists in Europe. The ethnic or religious status of the members of the salon did not matter because it was the uniqueness of character and personality that gave many Jews an equal status within the salon. Arendt's discussion of this phenomenon foreshadows many of her conclusions in *The Origins of Totalitarianism*, since in spite of the fact that Varnhagen gains some notoriety with her salon and some acceptance by marrying and converting to Christianity, this strategy also exemplifies what put Jews at risk politically. Varnhagen and her contemporaries were not interested in gaining equal political rights, but in freeing themselves as special individuals who somehow escaped the stereotypes attached to the Jewish people. Arendt contends that many Jews struggled to be 'exception' Jews in which their Jewish ethnicity was excused because of their impressive talents, but Arendt sees this as a dangerous strategy, since their status as Jews is never fully accepted, but rather, covered over. As Mihály Vajda puts it, the desire to be an exception Jew means that you 'could be accepted only if you were *different from the Jews, as a Jew unlike a Jew*', which of course, does nothing to improve the perception of the Jews as a whole.[6] When Arendt was a small child, her mother taught her that if she was attacked by antisemites, she must defend herself (*PA* 9). As an adult, Arendt saw the wisdom of this approach and concluded that if attacked as a Jew one must defend oneself 'as a Jew', and never be ashamed of it (*PA* 12). The desire to hide one's Jewish background or assimilate entirely into society was often rooted in a sense of shame or deep-seated belief in the negative status of being Jewish. Arendt believes that one must fight to attain equal political status without apology and without an appeal to abstract universal notions of human rights which do not defend being Jewish, but make claims about humanity in abstraction from ethnicity or religion. In her book on Varnhagen, Arendt describes two different responses of European Jews during the nineteenth century to antisemitism and Rahel Varnhagen serves as an example of someone who is in the middle of these two types (*PA* 71). The Jew in general, who is not participating in 'exceptional' activities are pariahs, or persons who have an outsider status in Europe which allows them to battle antisemitism to a degree, so long as they are not reclusive and politically uninvolved. Parvenus, on the other hand, have attained a special social status, but do not have the character or manners to be fully accepted either. Parvenus seek social status by any means necessary and do not acknowledge any solidarity with the Jewish people. As either pariahs or parvenus, the Jewish people were not accepted in Europe, and for Arendt, their pariah or parvenu status was an important factor that opened the door for rampant antisemitism in the beginning of the twentieth century.

Imperialism in Africa is the further factor that contributes to the possibility of totalitarian thinking. Arendt views imperialism as a preparatory stage for the rise of totalitarianism in Europe since it advocates the conquest of the world through the justification of race-thinking (*OT* 123).[7] This is not to say that racism did not exist in Europe prior to the nineteenth century, but Arendt claims that it did not exist as a monopolizing political ideology (*OT* 183). Arendt believes imperialist policies that sought to increase the wealth of the colonists needed race-thinking for justification. Imperialism differs from empire building like that of the Romans, because it does not include foreign peoples into the nation after they are conquered. One could not possibly rationalize the domination foreign lands and peoples to such an extent without some sort of belief in racial superiority. The colonists, like the Boers, saw themselves as men of adventure and saw the native peoples as savages who behaved similarly to nature. Therefore, there was no recognition of the pain or suffering caused, as the natives were treated like raw material whose labor could be used. The popularity of race-thinking took further hold after the fall of the aristocracy in Europe by replacing the aristocratic hierarchies, with racial ones. Race-thinking provided the bourgeoisie with a new type of natural hierarchy that justified the authority and elitism of the bourgeoisie in society through racial categories (*OT* 173).

For Arendt, the change from a political aristocracy into nation-states in the nineteenth century also led to the rise of totalitarianism.

The wealth of the middle class began to grow and it expanded into foreign imperialist investment which was motivated by a relationship of dependence, profit and exploitation. Arendt asserts that ironically, the bourgeoisie became politically emancipated through imperialism and colonialism because it allowed them to amass their wealth and increase their power without the help of the aristocracy (*OT* 138). This negatively affected the European Jews because they lost their important financial position in their relationship to the aristocracy. Nationalism was on the rise and since the Jews were not connected to a homeland and were 'rootless', it became easy to justify their different treatment. Within Germany, the downfall of the aristocracy and the formation of the nation-state resulted in political power becoming seated in the mob, rather than the people. Arendt believes that democratic type of government is better than an aristocratic monarchy, but this new kind of democracy needs to emerge under the right conditions. If the government does not allow for individuals to express themselves freely and honour the differences between persons, it can be just as damaging as a monarchy. Mob mentality does not promote individual free expression, but functions under mechanisms of conformity and sometimes, fear. Unfortunately, the mob always shouts for a strong man or leader and it became easy for the Jews to become the object of all that was detested in society.

What supplemented the growth of mob rule was the rise of the pan-national movements that began to grow throughout Europe, such as the pan-German movement originally started by Georg Von Schoenerer and Austrian students in Europe and the pan-Slavic movement occurring in Russia among the intelligentsia. Arendt calls these movements 'continental imperialism' because they sought expansion and power on the continent of Europe, rather than exploiting Africa or other parts of the world. The pan-national movements claim a type of divine 'chosen-ness' or origin to justify their superiority. Interestingly, these movements are not originally antisemitic, but the pan-Slavic movement turns antisemitic in 1881 according to Arendt, while the pan-German movement does not exclude Jews until 1918 (*OT* 239). After the First World War, the political climate was precarious. With high unemployment and inflation, a feeling of hostility arose with everyone against everyone else. When the bourgeoisie dominated class system began to fall apart, the masses rose up against the government, resulting in mob rule. The pan-national movements were hostile to the state and provided a political mechanism for the mob to express its outrage. This was preparatory for totalitarian thinking since for Arendt, totalitarianism involves resentment of the status quo and of government in general. Rather than focusing on national needs, totalitarian regimes view themselves as global movements that surpass the needs of isolated nations. The masses were guided by an attitude of both gullibility and cynicism because they trusted the pan-nationalist movement, but distrusted government generally (*OT* 382). By the 1920s and 1930s pan-national movements promoted antisemitism internationally and in Germany, pursued the goal of the eradication of the Jewish people.

The first two sections of *The Origins of Totalitarianism* are the most controversial of the book because sweeping historical and sociological claims are made by Arendt. The lengthy discussion of parts one and two on antisemitism and imperialism describe different occurrences from a variety of sources in order to show how race-thinking begins to emerge throughout the whole of Europe. Many of Arendt's claims are contentious, fail to make thorough connections to Stalinism, and none of what she says about African imperialism is based on first-hand evidence, unlike her discussions of antisemitism. However, while she spends the bulk of the book describing a sociological history of the conditions leading up to totalitarianism, the overall significance of Arendt's book has largely to do with the portions that describe totalitarianism itself.

TOTALITARIANISM

Hannah Arendt believes that totalitarianism is a new type of political formation that is unprecedented and differs from other kinds of political tyrannies. In fact, Arendt thinks that totalitarianism defies comparison because it explodes the traditional Western concepts of politics and government and calls for new ways of understanding (*EU* 339). In order to describe totalitarianism, Arendt makes some distinctions between totalitarianism and other forms of political tyranny or despotisms. The first difference between totalitarianism and tyranny is that typical political tyrannies invade other countries in order to gain material goods and land to increase the power of the tyrannical ruler. In tyrannies, people are dominated because of the self-interest of the ruler or group who seek to amass their power. Totalitarian regimes similarly involve a strong ruler like tyrannies, but the ruler does not primarily seek personal and selfish acclaim and power. In totalitarianism, invasion occurs primarily to promote the ideology of the regime, rather than the personal gain of the ruler. In the case of Nazism, this ideology concerns a racist dogma promoting the prominence of the Aryan race, while for Stalinism, the ideology concerns the need to eradicate capitalism and the bourgeoisie. The totalitarian ruler promotes the ideology of the government and justifies all actions according to it, even at the expense of the resources of the regime or the nation. The totalitarian ideology functions by dividing the world into two hostile forces battling each other for global dominance and turns the fight of the enemy into a worldwide fight to combat the global conspiracies of the enemy (*OT* 367). The goal is to destroy the enemy completely and terror techniques are justified as proper methods for containing the enemy. In contrast to tyrannies, the goals of totalitarianism are global in scope and move beyond the nationalistic enterprises. These ideological goals are more important than anything else and the regime will even risk its own demise in order to promote them. One example of the non-utilitarian nature of totalitarianism is Hitler's use of the death camps. While the labor of those sentenced to death could have been used in the war effort and the cost to create and maintain the camps could have been used to finance battle at the front lines, Hitler chose to sacrifice national interests for the larger global concern of the ideology. For Arendt, the gas chambers 'did not benefit anybody', since they were a costly endeavour that took up troops, rail transportation and other financial resources (*EU* 236). Tyrannies are utilitarian and pragmatic in accruing power for the ruler, but totalitarian governments sacrifice personal or national self-interest for the sake of the ideology.

The second way that totalitarianism differs from other sorts of political tyrannies is that not only is it non-utilitarian in its aims, but totalitarianism also lacks a practical and hierarchical structure that is typical of tyrannies. Tyrannies have a strict and understandable hierarchy, with the despot functioning as the top level of power and each action that is taken is perceived to be useful and in the interest of the dominant ruler. Conversely, totalitarian governments function without a clear-cut hierarchy, but with multiple levels of administration and bureaucracy. Many of the branches of government have duplicate tasks and one can never tell which organization will rise within the overall movement. This flexible and mobile movement lacks structure that allows for power to remain up for grabs. Stephen J. Whitfield describes this ordering of government as 'whirl' which is intended to keep everyone off balance, as opposed to typical political structures that seek to stabilize government and power with order.[8] In totalitarianism, the secret police and various spying organizations add to the atmosphere of paranoia in which no one can be trusted and no one really knows what the other parts of the government are doing except for those who are in the highest levels of command. The state of ignorance concerning government operations protects the strong leader from being questioned by his underlings and with duplication existing within government, an organized opposition to the ruler never arises because persons are too busy fighting internally to increase the status of their own division to consider rebelling against the ruler (*OT* 404). The positions within the various branches of government continually shift, so that there is constant turnover and inclusion of the younger generations, which also means, that very few become particularly skilled or experienced at their jobs (*OT* 431). Since totalitarianism emerges in an atmosphere of economic worry, it provides endless duplicate jobs for its loyal members, with the result that every jobholder becomes an accomplice to the government (*OT* 432). Arendt describes the structure of totalitarianism as being like an onion, in which every layer protects the leader at the centre who has ultimate control (*OT* 413). This metaphor of the 'onion' captures the different overlapping layers of bureaucracy that protect the leader and insulate him from any kind of attack. Each layer only knows its own business and has great difficulty understanding the entirety of the onion as a whole.

Finally, totalitarianism differs from other kinds of political despotisms because while terror is used in both types of political systems, tyrannies use terror as a means to an end in order to frighten opponents and squash dissent. Totalitarian ideologies use terror much more broadly, to rule masses of people who are perfectly obedient to the state, regardless of whether persons are actually public enemies of the regime (*OT* 6). In typical tyrannies and despotisms, persons who are outspoken against the regime are cruelly punished. In totalitarianism, it no longer matters if persons are actually guilty of the 'crime' of going against the government. The purpose of the police is altered from discovering and prosecuting crimes, to rounding up certain types of people that have been targeted by the ideology for imprisonment or elimination (*OT* 426). The victims are groups that are chosen randomly and declared to be unfit to live (OT 432). The torture that occurs has no aim, as information concerning guilt is not required to condemn the victims and re-education is perceived to be a waste of time (*OT* 453). Concentration camps arise to handle persons who are ultimately annihilated by the state. In an essay called 'Mankind and Terror', Arendt claims that a tyrannical government's use of violence can lead to a 'graveyard' of peace once dissent is contained through the use of force. Alternatively, there is no end to the terror in totalitarianism because the practical aim of stopping dissent is not the point (*EU* 299).

Typically, the purpose of modern government is viewed as promoting the common good of the people and if not the overall collective good, then at least governments are believed to be interested in securing and protecting the private, individual interests of the citizens. Totalitarianism clearly functions against the interests of the targeted groups in society, but additionally, even for those who appear friendly to the state, totalitarian regimes demand 'total, unrestricted, unconditional, and unalterable loyalty of the individual member', at the expense of their private concerns or interests, turning the purpose of government entirely upside down (*OT* 323). The intense loyalty of the members that is demanded at the cost of personal sacrifice is made possible by the feeling of isolation that totalitarianism promotes. Terror is used a tactic to enforce loyalty because persons are willing to turn friends into enemies in order to save themselves. This isolates individuals, since no one knows who can be trusted and free discussion of ideas is silenced. Because of the atmosphere of paranoia, Arendt believes that 'mutual suspicion . . . permeates all social relationships' even some of the most intimate family relations (*OT* 430). For Arendt, what is even more dangerous about the suspicion that pervades the community is that the citizens fear leaving the movement more than being held accountable for the crimes that they commit in the name of the movement (*OT* 373). This allows persons to commit all sort of brutal acts without feeling responsible for them, since they are ordered by the regime. Individual moral decision making can break down under these kinds of conditions. Totalitarian governments are worse than tyrannical governments that seek to undermine active critics through violence because totalitarianism takes away many of the means from which to think, question and challenge the state at all (*OT* 474).

Arendt believes that one reason that totalitarianism is effective and takes hold in communities is that common sense loses a grip on reality. Without being able to freely exchange ideas with other persons and by being completely isolated, the extreme goals of the movement are never checked by the reality of conditions. The totalitarian government presents a false face to the world and bases its ideology upon a global conspiracy that cannot be confirmed. Propaganda reinforces the ideology and it does not even matter if the party members believe the propaganda, so long as the capacity of distinguishing the difference between truth and falsehood is abolished in society (*OT* 385). Blocking out the external world of facts, the 'members live in a fool's paradise of normalcy' surrounded by sympathizers (*OT* 368). The leader is the only bridge to the outside world and he defends against it by filtering everything through his perspective. The lack of a need to regard the reality of the facts is extended to the operations of the secret police, who serve as the nucleus for power in these regimes, because they can imprison persons at will. Because the leader of the party is protected by onion-like layers of bureaucracy and administration, the totalitarian regime produces its own protected world that never needs to deal with what exists outside of the onion and has no way of checking the facts against what the layers of bureaucracy are producing. The key is that the ruler is granted the status of 'unending infallibility', in which facts will be denied, distorted or destroyed in order to secure the 'truth' of the ideology (*OT* 349). It is the consistency of the system that matters, not necessarily the individual facts, so the onion-like structure of the totalitarian regime seeks to reproduce a consistent picture and if the facts do not agree with the official fiction, the facts are treated as non-facts (*OT* xxxii). Arendt believes that at the root of totalitarian communities is a lack of common sense among the members and the ability to accept dubious 'facts'. Since there is no free exchange of ideas, the ability of the common sense to sort out the facts is compromised by the totalitarian forces that maintain the 'lying world of consistency' (*OT* 353).

The overall effect of totalitarian governments is that they prevent freedom and spontaneous political action from occurring. By promoting an atmosphere in which no one can be trusted and by isolating individuals from one another, no one is comfortable expressing their political views or acting against the regime, since it will result in imprisonment or death. The uniqueness inherent in each person's perspective on government is ignored and eliminated from the public sphere. Persons have difficulty producing political convictions as they are left isolated and unable to truly reflect on their situation. Arendt believes that the most dangerous aspect of totalitarianism is that it treats individuals as if they are superfluous. Individuals are no longer unique and important contributors to culture and politics, but creatures that can be easily sacrificed for the ideology or be conditioned to act in a predictable and obedient manner to cohere with the ideology. Because of the promotion of the superfluity of humanity, Arendt originally characterizes totalitarianism as a form of 'radical evil', a term that she borrows from Kant, but alters its meaning from the Kantian use. For Kant, radical evil occurs when an individual consistently chooses immorality, rather than trying to follow the moral law.[9] For Arendt, radical evil involves the belief that humans are superfluous and expendable (*OT* 459). Particularly, the use of concentration camps by both the Nazis and the Bolshevists exemplifies the belief in the superfluity or expendability of human life. The camps that arise in totalitarian regimes are isolated and seek to establish that the targeted groups of people never really existed, were never meant to exist, as if they were already dead (*OT* 445). Arendt asserts that the unique identity of the individual is destroyed long before life is actually taken through various dehumanizing measures like the shaving of heads, packing people into cattle cars and giving them camp clothing. Then the victims are further tortured by being given jobs in the administration of the camp, effectively blurring the line between being a victimizer and being a victim (*OT* 452–3). The chance of becoming a martyr becomes impossible, since no one will know of any heroic acts that occur in the camps. Arendt thinks that there were very few documented revolts in the camps because through the dehumanization process, the possibility of human spontaneity and freedom is destroyed (*OT* 455). Dehumanization targets the species and animal nature of humanity in which humans are expected to act like preprogrammed things or marionettes (*OT* 457). For Arendt, the dehumanization of the camps reduces humans to behaving predictably, like Pavlov's dogs (*EU* 242). While Arendt does not believe that humans have an essential and determined nature, she does believe that it is *like* the nature of humanity changes in totalitarianism because the freedom to act politically, which is a specifically human trait, is crushed, allowing totalitarianism to perpetuate.

Due to their sweeping ideologies, totalitarian movements are effective so long as they continue to expand on their global mission and promote their cause worldwide. Fortunately, these movements end when the leader who sits at the centre of the onion dies and their perceived infallibility and power cease to exist. Totalitarian regimes promote the idea that some humans, namely, the powerful rulers, have access to the truth of the ideology which is connected to the 'secret' operations of history or nature, while at the same time, they deny the political potential of the average individual. The leader represents the ideology and is thought to be able to make his or her will manifest in the world by assisting nature and history. The sweeping claims concerning history and nature serve as the engine for driving the movement forward and provide the motivation for both the ideology and terror of totalitarianism.

TOTALITARIANISM, NATURE AND HISTORY

In *The Origins of Totalitarianism*, and particularly in her revised ending called 'Ideology and Terror', Hannah Arendt critiques the relationship between totalitarianism and certain theories of history or nature, and she repeats this criticism often throughout the rest of her work. For Arendt, the problem begins with modern teleological theories of history, or theories that assert that human history is a universal process that is moving towards a specific end, aim or purpose, called a *telos* in Greek. The central idea in teleological theories of history is the human species is progressing throughout history and improving over time. While Arendt claims that originally, theories of human progress mainly concerned the education of humanity that passed down knowledge from generation to generation, she believes in the late eighteenth and early nineteenth centuries, these theories of history become more robust. Particularly, the theories of Hegel and Marx are significant because they assert that there is not only an end to history, but that it is possible for present day humans to know the content of that end. Arendt finds Karl Marx's theory to be of particular importance since Marx further suggests that something can be done currently in order to hasten the end, which in the case of Marx, involves the emancipation of the worker. History is believed to be something that can be managed, controlled and concerns the future, rather than just the past. These theories encourage humans to act now to bring about the end of history and imply a future politics, rather than just summarizing events of the past. Within totalitarian movements of the twentieth century, theories of history and nature are taken to additional extremes, according to Arendt. The ideology of totalitarian regimes is connected in significant ways to theories of history and nature and the belief that the leaders can gain access to and control of their secrets (*OT* 461–2).

Unlike teleological theories of history that focus on attaining a specific end, totalitarian theories of history or nature concentrate on understanding the movement and process of history or nature, rather than the goal. Whatever science can discover through repeating a process is considered a good, even if the information could be used to annihilate the human species, as in the case of nuclear technology. This interest in processes that can be made by human beings simultaneously applies to the realm of human affairs and history in the twentieth century because the key concepts used to understand them are also 'development' and 'progress' (*BPF* 61). History is thought to concern how historical processes come into being and how they can be controlled and reproduced. Consequently, humans are no longer content with the role of the observers, but alter what was once considered to be 'natural' or 'historical' processes, into processes that can be fabricated by human beings (*HC* 231). The fabrication of the processes of history or nature at their extreme is the methodology of totalitarian regimes. In Nazism, the ideology centres around access to the secrets of nature, while for Stalinism, the ideology concentrates upon the secrets of history. Arendt calls the relationship between totalitarian view of nature and history 'acting into nature', and 'acting into history' to signify the political effect of these ideological beliefs.

In *The Origins of Totalitarianism*, Arendt describes Nazism as a totalitarian regime guided by a fabrication of the law of nature because of its commitment to the infinite creation of a purified race of human beings.[10] The goal is to assist the process of nature in order to maintain the law of nature that has somehow failed to maintain itself. Alternatively, she describes Stalinism as driven by a fabrication of the law of history because of its commitment to the infinite creation of a Marxist/Stalinist society. For Arendt, the way that totalitarianism functions is that it places unsurpassed power in the hands of a single individual or ruler who sacrifices immediate interests for some extreme and fictitious reality to be actualized in an ever distant future (*OT* 412). The point is to accelerate the laws as quickly and expansively as possible. For Arendt, 'dying classes or decadent races on which history and nature have . . . passed judgment will be the first to be handed over to the destruction already decreed for them' (*EU* 306). The idea of killing certain portions of the society becomes possible because they are deemed to be already in decline. Arendt states:

> If you believe in earnest that the bourgeoisie is not simply antagonistic to the interests of the work, but is dying, then evidently you are permitted to kill all bourgeois. If you take literally the dictum that the Jews, far from merely being the enemies of other people, are actually vermin, created as vermin by nature and therefore predestined to suffer the same fate as lice and bedbugs, then you have established a perfect argument for their extermination. (*EU* 355)

In both Nazism and Stalinism, the focus is on the process of history or nature, and not on the end, because the end will never be accomplished. If the short-term aims of either of these regimes are achieved, new categories of persons would be found to be unfit to live or new economic classes of persons would be persecuted. Ultimately, the fabrication of the process of history or nature aims to fabricate humanity itself. According to Arendt, totalitarianism

> executes the law of History or of Nature without translating it into standards of right and wrong for individual behavior. It applies the law directly to mankind without bothering with the behavior of men. The law of Nature or the law of History, if properly executed, is expected to produce mankind as its end product; and this expectation lies behind the claim to global rule for all totalitarian governments. Totalitarian policy claims to transform the human species into an active unfailing carrier of a law to which human beings otherwise would only passively and reluctantly be subjected. (*OT* 462)

The fabrication of processes of history and nature that are intended to demonstrate the increased power and control of certain human beings, only serve to fabricate and dominate human beings themselves.

For Arendt, average citizens become cogs in the machine of historical or natural progress in totalitarianism, as their significance to the movement is only in service of the ideology (*OT* 329). Totalitarian regimes insist upon the infallibility of the strong leader to control society and history, while likewise maintaining the powerlessness of the average person. For the regime to succeed, it must keep moving and expanding towards its never ending goal, while sacrificing everything for the ideology. Arendt calls the scientific and historical laws of totalitarian regimes 'pseudo-science', since they are not based on anything that can be questioned and all evidence to the contrary is ignored (*OT* 468). The ideology provides a straight jacket of thought that does not encourage people to freely question the regime, because the supreme idea is meant to explain everything, making it very challenging for the average person to fight back (*OT* 470). The atmosphere of paranoia and fear discourages free political action and aims at putting an end to any dissent. Therefore, when totalitarian movements take hold, it is extremely difficult to end them, unless the leader is somehow removed or killed.

Arendt's own theory of history arises in sharp contrast to totalitarian ideology. Arendt thinks of history in terms of narratives or stories that remember the actions of unique individuals and give meaning to them for the community. Arendt traces the origin of history in general to the importance of legends for a community. Legends, for Arendt, are meaningful because they explain the true significance of an event to a community. Legends are not factual representations of what occurred in the past, but they serve as 'belated corrections of facts and real events', because they underscore the true meaning of the event to the community, regardless of the facts of the matter (*OT* 208). Arendt believes that the prepolitical and prehistorical condition of history is the fact that 'every individual life between birth and death can eventually be told as a story with beginning and end' and after death, all that remains of a life are the stories that others can tell about that person (*PA* 180). The stories or narrations of action can also be reified into materials and can become fabricated objects that are historically significant to a community. Arendt classifies the historian, the poet, the artist, the writer and the monument builder as examples of persons who construct narratives about the past that can disclose human action (*HC* 173). Historical narratives can be constructed because political actions always produce stories that are created retrospectively and these stories can be shared publicly.[11] Historical narratives also do not tell the conclusive tale of a person's actions once and for all. The story of the action can be reworked and the meaning of it can change over time (*MDT* 21). Since the meaning of the story can be revised, Arendt believes storytelling 'reveals meaning without committing the error of defining it' and allows for different interpretations of the meaning of an action in the future (*MDT* 105). Lisa Jane Disch describes Arendt's use of historical 'storytelling' as a form of critical thinking, which neither makes claims to a privileged vantage point of truth, nor discusses history in terms of inevitability.[12] Storytelling allows a community to come to terms with free political action of the citizens without having to invent an explanation concerning the aims or processes of history. In contrast to teleological versions of history, human dignity is restored because human beings are the ultimate judgers of history and history is not decided by invisible historical or natural forces behind our backs. In contrast to totalitarian versions of history, Arendt's view of history celebrates individual acts and does not treat the individual as superfluous, but as an important contributor to a community.

Arendt prefers this form of history based upon narrative and storytelling to a philosophy of history that gives a definitive end or purpose to history. Arendt is fond of a quotation from Isak Dinesen which states 'all sorrows can be borne if you put them into a story or tell a story about them' (qtd in *MDT* 104). Through the story, a meaning is revealed concerning suffering which would otherwise 'remain an unbearable sequence of sheer happenings' (*MDT* 104). In teleological and totalitarian theories of history, negative events can be justified as unfortunate, but necessary, side-effects due to the grand scheme of history. Thus, the individual is sacrificed to the aims of history or nature. In fact, whole segments of society can be killed in order to make the way for the ideological laws of nature or history. Arendt's narrative does not set the aims to history, but interprets action after the fact. Through a theory of history as narrative, Arendt maintains meaning for individual events without constructing a meta-narrative and avoids the hubristic sense of control at the heart of totalitarian theories of history or nature.

In her next books, Hannah Arendt describes positive political concepts that are meant to encourage differences of opinion, celebrate individuality and counteract the totalitarian ideology that she is so adamantly against. Her political theory will be described in the next chapter. However, after Arendt writes the elements of her positive theory of political action, she revisits totalitarianism again from a different angle in order to explain the mental processes of citizens living within a totalitarian state. She wants to understand not only how totalitarian infrastructure works, and how it develops historically, but also how it influences the way the citizens think. In short, she wants to understand why so many persons went along with the immorality of the actions demanded by the Nazi regime. Her opportunity to explore this problem arose in 1961 when she attended Adolf Eichmann's trial in Jerusalem in order to cover it for *The New Yorker*. Her findings throughout the trial supplement her entire theory of totalitarianism by explaining how totalitarianism influences the mind of a mid-level official during the Nazi regime.

THE BANALITY OF EVIL

In the years between *The Origins of Totalitarianism* and *Eichmann in Jerusalem*, Arendt realized that understanding the way a person thinks when living under and agreeing with a totalitarian ideology is crucial to understanding how such senseless movements established power in Germany and Russia. In *The Origins of Totalitarianism*, Arendt says that she consciously left out the memoirs of the Nazi generals that were available because she thought they displayed a lack of comprehension concerning the political facts of the matter (*OT* xxviii). Interestingly, in her later book from 1963, Arendt considers Adolf Eichmann's account during his trial in order to understand the thought process involved with those who changed from somewhat average citizens into persons who actively participated in the mass killings of other citizens. Arendt states that she accepted the assignment to cover Eichmann's trial because she wanted to confront an actual person, rather than to discuss a 'type' like in *The Origins of Totalitarianism*. She wanted to discover what motivated Eichmann to act as he did, to understand if Eichmann thought any of his actions were wrong, and to find out to what degree the traditional legal system could handle criminality under totalitarianism (*JW* 475). The Eichmann trial gave Arendt an opportunity to examine the impact of totalitarian ideology on criminality of a specific individual.

The conclusions that Arendt drew in *Eichmann in Jerusalem* mark a shift in her description of how totalitarianism functions and gains power. In *The Origins of Totalitarianism* and other works, Arendt describes the notion of 'radical evil' that occurred in the death camps which involved the belief in the superfluity of certain humans. Her description of the case of Eichmann painted a different picture. Arendt's experience of the trial promoted the conclusion that Eichmann was not an evil, wicked, calculating, sadistic monster. As a Jew herself, this was not a popular position to take on Eichmann, but what Arendt learned is that totalitarian regimes did not necessarily produce evil monsters. What they often produce were persons who were unable to think for themselves and unable to understand the wrongness of their actions, given that everything they did was sanctioned by law and supported by the regime in power. Arendt calls this situation the 'banality of evil'. Evil is not banal because it is unimportant, but because it can occur without diabolical intent and is often the result of massive failure of thought. For Arendt, totalitarianism promotes a breakdown in the way persons think and Eichmann is a good example of someone who was deluded about his actions. Caring more about the ideology than what is actually happening in the world, Eichmann let the Nazi ideology make his decisions for him and distanced himself from the consequences of his actions.

Arendt claims that the evidence for her new conclusion was drawn from Eichmann's testimony. During the trial in 1961, what struck Arendt about Eichmann was his reliance on stock phrases and clichés that he repeated over and over, word for word, in order to explain why he followed orders (*EJ* 44). Arendt thinks that such startling self-deception was exhibited throughout German society during the Nazi regime and Arendt points to slogans for the war, like calling it 'the battle for the destiny of the German people', as an example of such self-deception. This phrase allows persons to distance themselves from what was really happening in a number of ways. First, those who are actively engaged with the war could assert that it was not a typical war, but more of an ideological war (*EJ* 47). Second, the Germans could believe that they had not started the war, but destiny did and that the war was preordained by history and not really an act of aggression by the Germans (*EJ* 47). Third, it suggests that it was a matter of life and death for the Germans, and really, an act of self-defence (*EJ* 47). The rhetoric that permeated the culture allowed persons to justify their criminal actions and avoid responsibility for them.

Arendt found Eichmann to be unintelligent, but his most significant character flaw was that he was unable to look at anything from another person's point of view (*EJ* 43). This failure to imagine the perspectives of others contributed to his insensitivity and ability to take part in the brutal policies of the Nazis. In addition, Arendt found Eichmann's critical thinking skills, particularly in cases of moral decision making, to be intentionally lacking. Arendt described

Eichmann's language as 'officialese' and Eichmann's deficiency was not a question of mere intelligence, but concerned Eichmann's unwillingness to engage with moral thought and question the ideology of the state. Not only did Eichmann fail to question Nazi ideology, but he defended his immoral actions as working within the law and doing his best to fulfil his duty to obey the law (*EJ* 120). At times, Eichmann claimed that it was a struggle to follow his duty and he had the audacity to compare this with the struggle to follow the moral law. He even thought of himself as a type of Kantian ethicist, but the problem was the way in which Eichmann interpreted Kant's idea of moral duty. Whereas Kant believes that it is a duty to obey the moral law, Eichmann thought that it was a duty to obey the Führer's law and he did not take into consideration the morality of the requests (*EJ* 121). According to Larry May, the institutionalization of the multiple levels of bureaucracy in totalitarian regimes socializes unthinking administrators to follow orders and feel exempted from the responsibility of their actions because they felt passively acted upon, rather than actively participating in the acts.[13] The Nazi administrators began to view themselves as going beyond the call of duty and suffering to fulfil the goals of the regime, rather than actively making the goals arise in the world.

Startlingly, during the trial, Eichmann claimed not to be a Jew-hater and ultimately viewed himself as innocent because he never actually killed anyone and never directly gave an order to a subordinate to kill (*EJ* 19). Eichmann was in charge of emigration, including the transportation of the Jews and other groups to the death camps, so he felt that he was not directly implicated in their deaths, since he merely transported them. Eichmann claimed that when the level of the violence of the final solution began to be revealed to mid-level officials like him, he was genuinely surprised by the violence inherent in the solution (*EJ* 79). Yet, he grew to accept the solution after attending meetings where no one in authority questioned the policy, and in comparison to the more powerful leaders, Eichmann did not think he was in a position to judge the policy (*EJ* 101). In fact, Eichmann seemed to agree with other Nazi officials that he was being generous to the Jews and other victims because the gas chambers allowed for a more charitable way to die than other forms of execution (*EJ* 96). Though he displayed one moment of heroism, by redirecting a train of gypsies from a concentration camp to a place where they would be allowed to live, he got in trouble for the act and never attempted it again (*EJ* 88). He grew to accept the policy and enforce the policy, ultimately failing to see what was wrong with it in the first place.

What is significant about Arendt's theory concerning the 'banality' of evil is that evil political acts are not always committed by monsters, but can occur through extreme insensitivity and lack of reflection, even among persons who are not particularly evil at the start. As Norma Claire Moruzzi notes, persons are likely to shirk the work of thinking, even in the best of times, which becomes more pronounced in extreme situations, and leaves them open to totalitarian policies.[14] The problem for Arendt is that people become so focused on finding the monsters that they fail to notice how many people had major lapses in moral thinking under totalitarian rule. In a totalitarian society that actively promotes the lack of critical thinking skills, persons are apt to cling to codes or rules of conduct. The danger for those who rely on codes of conduct, rather than their own judgment, is that that a totalitarian regime can change the content of the codes of conduct at any moment and the new policy gains acceptance since the moral knowledge necessary to evaluate the change is lacking for many (*RJ* 178). Arendt feels that it would be comforting to believe that Eichmann is a sadistic monster because then one could consider his behaviour to be an isolated incident (*EJ* 253). What is truly frightening for Arendt is that Eichmann is 'terrifyingly normal', and he signifies a new type of criminal for which knowledge of right and wrong is lacking (*EJ* 253). Totalitarianism produces a new type of criminal for Arendt, one that does not murder in order to murder, but murders as part of his or her career (*JW* 487). By framing the question of political evil in terms of banality, Arendt urges a change in focus, away from concentrating on the evil monsters of the world, to see the new kind of criminals who do not even know that what they are doing is wrong. Many interpret Arendt's doctrine of the banality of evil as suggesting that there is an 'Eichmann' in each of us that could emerge given the right totalitarian conditions. Arendt denies this view because she thinks that his actions were extreme and that he is responsible for them, including his lack of concern for others. Arendt claims that the only distinguishing characteristic of someone like Eichmann is 'perhaps extraordinary shallowness' (*RJ* 159). This realization concerning the banality of evil motivated Arendt to examine the contemplative life and political judgment in her final work, called *The Life of the Mind*. Political judgment is one of the faculties that atrophies in totalitarianism and will be discussed in Chapter four.[15]

Some scholars have noted that the change from radical evil to banality of evil is one of the few areas in which Arendt changed her mind over the years. Arendt herself admits in a response to her critic, Gershom Scholem, that she had changed her mind and no longer uses the term 'radical evil' (*PA* 396). She states:

> It is indeed my opinion now that evil is never 'radical,' that it is only extreme, and that it possesses neither depth nor demonic dimension. It can overgrow and lay waste the whole world precisely because it spreads like a fungus on the surface. It is 'thought-defying,' as I said, because thought tries to reach some depth, to go to the roots, and the moment it concerns itself with evil, it is frustrated because there is nothing. That is its 'banality'. (*PA* 396)

Yet, perhaps the greatest difference between the two perspectives on totalitarianism concerns the role of ideology on the individual. In a letter to her friend Mary McCarthy, Arendt claims that she may have 'overrated the impact of ideology on the individual' in *The Origins of Totalitarianism* (*BF* 147). Arendt asserts that she did not see a sign of 'firm ideological convictions' in Eichmann, like a commitment to producing a more racially pure world, but rather, a lack of deep-rooted convictions about anything (*LM* 4). So while the ideology may be important for some level of philosophical justification for totalitarian regimes, it may not significantly affect the average mid-level official.

Despite Arendt's admission concerning her change of position on evil, Elisabeth Young-Bruehl, Margaret Canovan and Richard J. Bernstein all argue that radical and banal evil are compatible with one another and that the more recent doctrine of the 'banality of evil' merely supplements and expands upon her prior view. Given that totalitarianism works to promote the superfluity of individual persons, a description of evil as banal seems to encapsulate the superfluity of the individual inherent in the concept of radical evil. Elisabeth Young-Bruehl argues that when motives for evil are superfluous, then evil becomes banal, suggesting that banality is just a different word for the radical evil that she first articulated.[16] Richard J. Bernstein agrees by asserting that since Arendt is vague in defining radical evil, except for connecting it to superfluity, and since banality of evil is compatible with believing in the superfluity of humanity, he thinks that the ideas are not contradictory but are demonstrative of the fact that Arendt never truly believed in the Satanic quality of the Nazi's actions.[17] Bernstein maintains that there is a major shift in Arendt's emphasis from superfluity, to banality, but overall, does not see a drastic and opposite view being adopted by Arendt. Especially in her discussions of the bureaucratic onion of totalitarianism, there was always something passive, unthinking and banal concerning how evil occurs. However, it is clear that Arendt herself believes there is at least some difference between the two positions.

In general, what ultimately connects the two books on totalitarianism is that the lack of common sense and free thinking that is demonstrated in its extreme by Eichmann. In *The Origins of Totalitarianism*, Arendt claims that totalitarianism partly arises because freedom of thought and speech are denied and because of this, common sense loses its grasp on reality. The totalitarian ruler hides or makes unavailable the proof of the horrors committed by the regime, so even for the outside world, common sense refuses to believe what is actually occurring in the community (*OT* 437).[18] In addition, totalitarian regimes change the facts to suit the purposes of the regime and make it difficult for the average citizen to judge the ideology against reality, which is supplemented by the use of terror to further isolate and intimidate persons. Though Eichmann was one of the officials who was fully aware of the atrocities, he could simultaneously distance himself from his responsibility and from the immorality of the acts, which signalled a complete lack of common sense and moral judgment on his part. By having large portions of the society with a curtailed common sense, or restricted ability to adequately judge the political situation, it allowed for new mores to be easily adopted among these groups and promoted political passivity for those whose moral thinking was not as compromised.

Despite Arendt's analysis of Eichmann as someone who does not really know what he is doing, Arendt does not believe that Eichmann is innocent (*EJ* 254–6). Arendt closes *Eichmann in Jerusalem* by articulating what she thinks the courts should have said to him. Arendt does not believe in the collective guilt of the German people, because she sees this as a way to exempt the truly guilty. Arendt was against the concept of collective guilt in general because she thought that if 'all are guilty, no one is' (*RJ* 28). She claimed that even if 80 million

Germans are complicit with Nazism, it was not an excuse for Eichmann's behaviour (*EJ* 255). She states:

> We are concerned here only with what you did, and not with the possible noncriminal nature of your inner life and of your motives or with the criminal potentialities of those around you. You told your story in terms of a hard-luck story, and, knowing the circumstances, we are, up to a point, willing to grant you that under more favorable circumstances it is highly unlikely that you would ever have come before us or before any other criminal court. Let us assume, for the sake of argument, that it was nothing more than misfortune that made you a willing instrument in the organization of mass murder; there still remains the fact that you have carried out, and therefore actively supported, a policy of mass murder. For politics is not like the nursery; in politics obedience and support are the same. And just as you supported and carried out a policy of not wanting to share the earth with the Jewish people and the people of a number of other nations – as though you and your superiors had any right to determine who should and who should not inhabit the world – we find that no one, that is, no member of the human race, can be expected to want to share the earth with you. This is the reason, and the only reason, you must hang. (*EJ* 255–6)

Arendt thinks that Eichmann deserved the death penalty because he knowingly supported mass murder and he was accountable for the decision to fail to question the policy. Eichmann's defence was the defence of a child who blames the elders and society for his own actions. The idea of collective guilt allows for persons to deny responsibility for criminal acts.[19] Arendt's politics are designed to combat such passivity in citizens. Her politics encourage differences of opinion and active engagement in civic life. Most importantly, her view of politics honours the individuality and uniqueness of the human actor and is the opposite of a policy that regards citizens as superfluous.

CHAPTER TWO

PHILOSOPHICAL THOUGHT AND THE HUMAN CONDITION

The Human Condition (1958) is Arendt's most important book because it traces certain elements of Arendt's positive political philosophy.[1] Arendt's view of politics is designed to counter totalitarian politics, so rather than stressing conformity and silence in society, Arendt's work emphasizes differences of opinion and open debate. Unlike many of her philosophical predecessors, Arendt valorizes political action and explores the components of what she calls the *vita activa*, or the active life. It is Arendt's view that the tradition of philosophy tends to prioritize the life of philosophizing, or the contemplative life of the mind as the favoured type of life, which results in the stifling of the diversity in politics, since most political theorists argue for the one true set of political doctrines, rather than being open to the diversity of opinion in the public sphere. Focusing on the life of the mind, or the *vita contemplativa*, may shed insight upon philosophy and theory, but it is the improper emphasis for understanding politics which focuses on activity. In *The Human Condition*, Arendt describes the different components of the active life in contrast to the life of the mind to counterbalance the traditional overemphasis of contemplation and thinking in philosophy. Arendt does not assert that thinking is less important than politics, but her book is intended to make up for a lack of attention to political action by theorists (*HC* 17). In order to understand Arendt's views about the different components of the active life, it is important to first explore her precise criticisms of the philosophical tradition, especially how the emphasis on contemplation and thinking pushes politics in a more tyrannical direction. Dana Villa calls *The Human Condition* a work in which Arendt wars against philosophy and it is necessary to appreciate Arendt's worries about philosophy in order to understand her positive political claims.[2]

PHILOSOPHY AND POLITICS

Though the tragedy of the Holocaust is unthinkable to many of us, one reason why this fact was particularly unfathomable to Arendt was that she was a philosophy graduate student during the war. At the time, Germany was at the forefront of the philosophical world and Arendt was shaken by the fact that the immense intelligence of some of the members of the German academy did not help them to strongly criticize the atrocities of National Socialism. In fact, some intellectuals were members of the Nazi party and failed to have the common sense required to recognize the fascist and brutal nature of the movement. Margaret Betz Hull believes Arendt's frustration with traditional philosophy is grounded in the personal experience of the war and seeing the 'professional thinkers' get lost in the ivory tower of thought, while the world was falling apart politically.[3]

In *The Origins of Totalitarianism* and some of her early essays, Arendt asserts that European intellectual tradition did not influence the rise of totalitarianism in Europe, but Arendt later amends her view.[4] By the time of *The Human Condition*, Arendt had already written several articles that asserted that the study of philosophy was somewhat implicated in the rise of National Socialism through its failure to respond politically and through its tendency to advocate tyrannical forms of politics. Since philosophical thought and reflection on metaphysical questions require solitude, one political danger of the profession of philosophy is to be lost in seclusion and think of politics as a way to protect the solitude necessary for their work and to secure the freedom to refrain from politics altogether (*EU* 360). As a result of such indifference to important political concerns, Arendt rejects the title of philosopher in favour of the title political theorist throughout her life.

'Philosophy and Politics' is an essay that was initially part of a lecture series given at Notre Dame by Arendt in 1954, that examines the relationship between philosophy and politics established by ancient Greek philosophers like Plato and Aristotle. For Arendt, Plato is the one who is primarily responsible for emphasizing a contemplative approach and for turning politics into something that is based upon copying a universal theory. While Arendt has enormous criticisms of

Platonism in particular, her interpretation of ancient Greek thought is certainly not entirely negative and certain basic features of her political theory are inspired by the ancient Greek *polis* of Athens. But it is with the onset of philosophical thinkers like Plato, that the Greek interpretation of the political life begins to fail in Arendt's view. Arendt believes the problem with Greek political philosophy is that the role of the philosopher is misunderstood and as a result, the relationship between Western philosophy and politics continues to be tarnished.[5]

Arendt charges that beginning with Plato, the importance of political action has been ignored, in favour of political theorizing that constructs the ideal state intellectually and then seeks to copy this ideal construct in the real world. In Jacques Taminiaux's book titled *The Thracian Maid and the Political Thinker*, Taminiaux argues that the whole of Arendt's thought can be explained through a metaphor that she uses in her last major work, *The Life of the Mind*. Arendt describes a story told by Plato in *Theatetus* of the Thracian maid who laughs at the philosopher Thales. Thales was so concerned with looking at the stars in the heavens above, that he tripped and fell into a well.[6] Similarly, in her own assessment of the war, Arendt saw brilliant intellectuals, like Martin Heidegger, who were so concerned with deep theories of ontology and metaphysics that they thought were more fundamental than practical politics that they failed to recognize when political injustices were dominating society.[7] While this problem of inattention to the political is not specific to Plato's theory, but actually persists throughout a great deal of philosophical theory for Arendt, the way that Plato and to a lesser extent Aristotle, modelled how politics should be theorized and set the ground work for the tradition to consistently ignore politics and to think of politics primarily from a theoretical, rather than practical, viewpoint.[8]

In 'Philosophy and Politics', Arendt has two basic complaints with Plato's theory of politics and the first concerns the way in which Plato set the example for how political philosophy was to be done. For Arendt, Plato's main political theory comes from the *Republic*, which is a work that describes the most just political community. Plato describes the republic as being grounded in his famous theory of the forms which assumes that intellectual and perfect truths of knowledge can be attained and that these ideas are ontologically superior to the changeable objects of this world. The forms are perfect, godlike blue prints or patterns for an object or concept that define the essence of a thing and are unchanging, true ideas. For example,

Plato thinks that an object, like a chair, participates in the form of the chair or the perfect idea of 'chair-ness' that makes all chairs what they are. Similarly, the perfect political community is meant to participate in the form of the good and Plato describes this utopian community in the *Republic*. Plato believes that politics should be based on universal philosophical truths that can be conceived of in advance in order to realize them in the world. The *Republic* serves as a blueprint for that utopian community, as it contains the theory that needs to be enacted in the world. In fact, for Plato, it is actually the philosophers who rule the state because they are the ones who understand the true ideas of the good, justice and politics generally. Arendt thinks that Plato's theory impacts the study of politics because subsequent political philosophers follow the model that intellectual theory comes prior to and should guide the practice of politics and that political communities should be based upon universal and true philosophical ideas. The role of the philosopher is to articulate the truths of politics with the goal of making them happen in the world by convincing others of their merit. Alternatively, Arendt develops a political theory that is not based upon some preconceived idea of the just, but takes into account the different members of the community and their different perspectives concerning what should be done. For Arendt, it is tyrannical and anti-democratic to construct politics in advance without consulting the people to which it will apply.

The belief that politics can be understood according to universal and true ideas has resulted in a second problem, according to Arendt, because it has led to the political realm being theorized exclusively from the point of view of the philosopher, rather than taking the diverse perspectives of the people into account. It is Arendt's view that Plato's political theory arises in response to Socrates' execution for impiety and corruption of the youth, which significantly changes the relationship between philosophy and politics in Western thought. Arendt describes Plato's reaction to his mentor's execution as despair and dissatisfaction with politics because Socrates was unable to convince and persuade the Athenian citizens of the truth of his innocence.[9] From Plato's viewpoint, if the Athenians understood the 'Truth', they would not have executed Socrates. As a result, Plato denounces the concept of *doxa*, or opinion and opposes it to truth. For Plato, the trial was settled according to subjective opinions, rather than according to the truth and it led to the unjust killing of his friend. Plato decides that the philosopher kings, with philosophical knowledge of the forms, are the only ones qualified to rule because they alone are capable of insuring that the form of the good is approximated in practical politics. For Arendt, Plato serves as an example of someone who privileges the life of the philosopher and grants the philosopher the ability to rule the polis because he thinks it will prevent further injustices by those who are less qualified and do not know the truth of the forms. This is tyrannical because it ignores the importance of the opinions of other members of the community.

Arendt characterizes Plato's construal of politics as a distinct break from his predecessor, Socrates, who apparently fully understood the correct role of philosophy in relation to politics. Unlike Plato, Arendt argues that Socrates was not interested in the political implications of eternal philosophical truths like the forms, because he suspected that these truths were beyond the realm of human knowledge. According to Arendt, Plato's earlier, more Socratic, dialogues are evidence of Socrates' scepticism of truth, since these dialogues never attain a positive and conclusive answer or definition for the topic being discussed. Arendt believes that Socrates was not interested in truth, but he was interested in opinion, or *doxa*, which concerns the truth of the world as it opens to the individual. Arendt argues that Socrates understood that the *doxa* was 'the formulation in speech of what *dokei moi*, that is, what appears to me'.[10] The truth of the *doxa* is based on the understanding that although everyone experiences the same world, it opens itself differently to all persons, depending upon their position in it. Epistemologically, *doxa*, or opinion, is neither mere subjective fantasies, nor absolute truth that is valid for all.[11] *Doxa* is in-between the subjective and the objective and concerns the truth of one's experience of the world. In an article called 'Truth and Politics', Arendt suggests that the crucial difference between truth and opinion is in 'their *mode of asserting validity*' (*PA* 555). Statements of truth coerce because there is something undeniable about them that is beyond disagreement or dispute, such as the statement 'the three angles of a triangle are equal to two angles of the square' (*PA* 555). This statement cannot be debated and seen from a political perspective, looks tyrannical and despotic (*PA* 555–6). In contrast, political opinions can be argued with or rejected, while factual truths cannot be argued away and exclude any type of debate (*PA* 556).

The problem with Platonic politics for Arendt is that *doxa* is relegated to the role of subjective opinion and is discounted from having any political validity. In contrast, Arendt claims that politics should involve the different *doxai* of all the members of the community in order to come to a decision based upon what is best for the community as a whole, rather than negating the differing perspectives of the citizens in favour of a universal politics. Politics that are derivative from universal truths presume an ultimate truth or standard by which to make political decisions, pushing all political communities toward a universally true system of politics, which leads to the tyranny of not allowing for the possibility of legitimate disagreement between perspectives. With the idea of universal philosophical truth guiding the political realm, Arendt believes that Platonic politics really concerns politics based on the *doxai* of the philosophers who rule the state according to their subjective concerns for a life that involves contemplating philosophical truth. In *Promise of Politics*, which contains the preparatory material for her book *The Human Condition*, Arendt asserts that Plato's effort to persuade the multitude about the truth of politics was really a case of forcing his own opinion upon the people, which is only another kind of rule by violence (*PP* 13). Arendt disagrees with Plato, asserting that politics that is based upon one idea of the true does an injustice to the different members of the community by devaluing their political beliefs into mere subjective opinions that can be ignored and is decidedly anti-democratic. Whereas Socrates understands that one cannot know a person's *doxa* beforehand and concentrates on revealing it to the citizens, Plato 'destroys the plurality of the human condition within himself', by running the state according to his own *doxa* and ignoring all the others (*PP* 37). For Arendt, the virtuous statesman is one who tries to understand as many viewpoints as possible, rather than imposing one's own world-view upon the state (*PP* 18). By distinguishing the role of the philosopher from that of the political actor, Arendt is not denigrating the life of the thinker in comparison to other forms of life, but she is challenging its historical priority. Because the focus of philosophy is theoretical and founded in contemplation, it tends to ignore the opinions of others and is an inappropriate mode of thought for political action. Other kinds of truths, like scientific or even philosophical truths, remain based in universality. The point is that politics, in order to avoid tyranny, must be willing take into account the multiple perspectives of the community and tolerate the contradictions arising between various viewpoints.

Arendt believes that in contrast to Plato's philosopher king, Socrates saw his task, and the task of the philosopher, as trying to help people pinpoint the truth of their *doxai* in order to clearly identify their true opinions. A person's *doxa* is not self-evident, because one may hold self-contradictory views, or be unable to articulate one's views on a particular topic clearly. Socrates saw the political role of the philosopher as being a pestering gadfly, or one who helps others to find the truth of their *doxai*, which could then be carried over to politics.[12] Though discussing issues as a gadfly, Arendt thinks that Socrates sought to make persons more truthful with themselves, rather than trying to dictate universal philosophical truths to them. Socrates, therefore, does not seek to destroy *doxa* or opinion in order to reveal the 'truth' like Plato, but he seeks to reveal '*doxa* in its own truthfulness'.[13] The philosopher assists politics by helping persons elucidate their *doxai*, but should avoid providing political models of the ideal state and certainly should not seek to rule the state. This idea is reflected in Arendt's claim that when she taught in the classroom, she had no interest in converting her students to any specific political viewpoint. Unlike the Platonic philosopher, Arendt did not instruct them what to think or how to act, because she claimed that instruction and learning arises from exchanging opinions with other people and should not be dictated from above.[14]

By negating the importance of *doxa* and theorizing the political realm according to universal truths, philosophers utilize the wrong type of knowledge for thinking about politics and the resulting universalism is tyrannical in Arendt's view because it will not admit legitimate contrary views. This should not be understood as a rejection of all claims to truth, or an embracing of relativism or subjectivism because as Wayne Allen notes, the ultimate point is to get persons to think for themselves, in a way that is true to their own experience.[15] Likewise, her view of political theory should not be confused with rejecting the existence of all universal truths outright. It is merely that politics requires listening to other people's opinions, while other kinds of activities require different types of thought. Through tracing the history of political theory and addressing some of its shortcomings, Arendt turns her attention in *The Human Condition* to a political topic that is typically ignored by philosophical theory: the active life. In tracing the conceptual history of human activity, Arendt seeks to restore the importance of the active life and to provide an alternative view of political theory that is not based upon the life of philosopher or the intellectual, but is more inclusive of the diversity of interests of the citizens as a whole.

THE *VITA ACTIVA*

Despite her criticisms of Platonic theory, Arendt returns to ancient Greece for inspiration for her own theory of politics. However, rather than searching the philosophical tradition for ideas about how the political realm should be theorized, Arendt returns to prephilosophical categories in order to recapture the importance of politics and the active life in democratic Athens. According to Arendt's biographer, Elisabeth Young-Bruehl, Arendt describes her philosophical method as a type of 'conceptual analysis' that traces the origins of concepts, much like Nietzsche's genealogical method.[16] By tracing concepts back to their historical origins, she analyses the political conditions that give rise to the concepts, measures how much the concept has changed over time and determines when conceptual confusion arose surrounding the concept.[17] Most of the discussion in *The Human Condition* concerns tracing the various components of the active life back to their conceptual origins in order to understand how concern with activity was sacrificed by the philosophical tradition for an almost exclusive focus on contemplation.

Arendt divides human activity into three fundamental categories: labor, work and action which occur in the spaces of the public and the private.[18] Labor and work occur privately, while political action occurs publicly. These activities of the *vita activa*, or the active life, are related to the corresponding conditions of human life, which are natality and mortality, earth, worldliness and plurality (*HC* 11).[19] Arendt's title for the book, *The Human Condition*, stresses the conditioned nature of humanity in contrast to the way in which totalitarian ideologies construe of their leaders as unconditioned and all powerful beings that can control the processes of history and nature.[20] By describing the activities of labor, work and action, Arendt argues for the importance of politics connected to the category of action that manifests human freedom and allows persons to express their *doxa*, or opinion, in public. Arendt also asserts that with modernity, some of these categories have been altered and have become blurred, to the detriment of politics. Her view is not to reinstate ancient Greek life, which certainly contained many political inequalities, but to use some of these earlier categories to emphasize the importance of politics and to point the way towards a politics that is anti-totalitarian. Arendt claims that she does not offer a conclusive and concrete answer to practical political problems in *The Human Condition*, because answers are found with others, but her book is a work of theory that merely tries to think through what we are doing (*HC* 5).

One of the first categories that Arendt discusses in *The Human Condition* are labor and work. While she acknowledges that in contemporary language, labor and work are often treated as interchangeable words, Arendt describes them as different and distinct activities. Claiming to trace these concepts back to ancient Athens, Arendt believes human labor is an activity that is concerned with the cyclical and repetitive biological needs of human life, involving growth, metabolism and decay. Labor produces food for survival, but its efforts are not sustained for long, because the food must be consumed within a given period of time before it perishes. Labor is cyclical and repetitive because whether the product of labor is eaten or left to rot, it is reabsorbed back into organic life and the process must begin again. Since its demands are continuous, labor does not have a specific beginning or end. Labor is not guided by a means-end rationale, but includes an overlapping of means and ends that cannot be permanently sated. The survival needs tackled by labor are endless, but those needs must be addressed in order for human life to be sustained. Arendt supports the ancient Greek view that construes of labor as being enslaved by necessity and a form of deprivation because a life of labor originally meant that one was deprived of public life (*HC* 83). In fact, Arendt believes that the unfortunate institution of slavery emerged from a desire to exclude labor from making any demands upon the upper classes at all (*HC* 84). Yet, Arendt notes that there can also be a blessing and joy in the activity of labor, by living within the cycles of nature and enjoying the pleasure of that kind of pursuit (*PA* 172). Arendt describes humans in their laboring aspect as *animal laborans*. Since animals are also subject to the demands of nature, this kind of human activity is closest to animal activity. Labor is a necessary precondition for politics because one's needs must be taken care of before it is possible to focus on political concerns, but the activity of labor is decisively different from the category of political action. Political action occurs publicly and allows for freedom, while labor concerns the necessity of the demands of nature that occur in private for Arendt.

Work, in contrast to labor, fabricates more permanent structures, such as shelter and furniture that allow persons to begin to separate from nature. In contrast to the endless, cyclical, necessities attended to by human labor, the world created by fabrication is somewhat independent from human beings and provides a space of durability and relative permanence that differs the fruits of labor that decay quite quickly (*HC* 94). Laboring produces products that are to be consumed, but the products of work are to be used and reused. By building a world of more stable objects, humans begin to escape some of the cyclical demands of nature, which changes the focus of life from sheer survival and allows for the possibility of politics.

Arendt believes that fabrication, or work, begins with an act of violence, by destroying some aspect of nature in order to use it as material for a project. After the material has been gathered, the fabrication is made according to the idea of an artist or craftsman and is constructed according to a means-end rationale through the utilization of technological thinking. A pattern, blueprint or idea guides the actualization of the end product and the excellence of the object is determined by how well the product mimics its conceptualization (*HC* 173). Unlike the activity of political action, workers can reverse the product of work if necessary (*HC* 139). The fabricator has control over the process and there is a degree of reversibility with fabrications because the worker can destroy the product and begin again if the product is not satisfactory. By providing stability against the natural world, fabrications allow for the creation of a public space which relates and separates individuals and makes political action possible.

Arendt describes the worker as *homo faber*, or humanity in its fabricating capacity. Unlike labor which is cyclical, work has a definite beginning and end and from the point of view of nature, work appears to be more destructive than labor since it must violently wrestle raw materials from the earth to make more stable objects, rather than returning the resources back to nature quickly like the products of labor (*PA* 175, *HC* 100). Work inspires the creation of tools and instruments in order to achieve its ends and some of these tools are used in labor as well. Labor is connected to worldlessness for Arendt since the human body concentrates on nothing more than remaining alive and humans remain imprisoned in the metabolism of nature (*HC* 115). In contrast, work builds a world and a home for humanity and gives persons shelter and safety from the unpredictable world of nature. Work can also create self-confidence and sense of achievement in humanity as they overcome the elements. *Homo faber* acts as 'lord and master' and has control over nature. The activity of work occurs in privacy, since the master workers must be alone with their ideas or blueprints to create in isolation, but later, workers must meet in the public market-place to exchange their goods (*HC* 160–1). Work is more public than labor, since work requires the exchange market for trade, while laboring occurs in the home or on privately owned lands. The exchange market is a public place, but it is not the political realm of action because it is governed by private interests and commerce, in contrast to politics that involves persons acting together for specific common goals. The products of work are also tangible and do not depend on the presence of others, unlike action and speech of politics that require the spectators to witness it (*HC* 95).

The final and most important category of human activity for Arendt is action, or *praxis*. Action concerns politics and involves humans in their freest capacity. Arendt believes that fundamentally, humans are born equal, but they are also unique individuals, which Arendt connects to what she calls human 'plurality'. Humans are the same because they are members of the human species, they share a common world, and they are equal. Humans are different from one another because they are all unique, distinct individuals and there are no two human beings who are exactly alike (*HC* 175). For Arendt, each human being who is born is like a miracle because she or he will not be like anyone else in existence.[21] Action involves natality, which is a concept that is connected to the miracle of birth and new beginnings. Arendt derives the concept of natality from St Augustine, who thinks that every person 'being created in the singular, is a new beginning by virtue of his birth' (*LOM* II, 109). As natals, humans are born to bring something new into the world and it is through political action in the form of words and deeds that human beings are able to distinguish themselves and disclose their individuality to the world. For this reason, action is like a second birth because it allows persons to begin something new and disclose who they are. The kind of distinction associated with plurality is not the same as 'otherness' that Arendt relates to the biological differences between all organic objects (*HC* 176). Only human beings can reveal their unique individuality to others through words and deeds, and for this reason, Arendt believes that political action is the activity that is most specifically human. Arendt writes in *The Human Condition* 'in acting and speaking, men show who they are, reveal actively their unique personal identities and thus make their appearance in the human world' (179). In contrast to work, that seeks to create tangible things in the world, action discloses who a person is, which Arendt describes as the beginning of *somebody*, not *something* (*HC* 177). What is revealed through action is not a predetermined essence of a person, as if she was an object, but *who*, rather than *what* someone is. The disclosure of the 'who' allows one to be remembered beyond his or her lifetime. Through oral and written record and tradition, an individual's action can be remembered beyond one's life span and a person can attain a degree of immortality. The prephilosophical Greeks, according to Arendt, honoured human plurality, devoted their lives to political action and sought to be immortalized in the narratives of the citizens, historians and artists, who witnessed their actions in public.

Action involves words and deeds and is closely connected to speech because through it, persons reveal their gifts, talents and even their shortcomings (*HC* 179). Adriana Cavarero describes this political aspect of speech as revealing a person's uniqueness, rather than communicating the truth about a political idea, like in Plato's politics.[22] Through acting in political contexts, persons reveal who they are, but Arendt notes that they cannot control the outcome of their action or what the spectators will think of the action. This is in contrast to fabrication in which the craftsman understands ahead of time what the object to be made is supposed to look like, what it will be used for and what the desired end is, which can also be reversed if the object fails to satisfy the end. Political action differs because actors make an attempt to solve a problem, make a speech, or act on a public matter and it is really up to the spectators to decide what to make of that action and what significance the action has for the community. Arendt believes that the disclosure of who someone is 'can almost never be achieved as a wilful purpose' and she thinks that the significance of people's actions can often remain hidden from the actors themselves (*HC* 179). Action requires the involvement of other persons who make sense of it and it must occur publicly, rather than privately, to have any significance at all. Arendt describes action as being like a type of performance, but reminds the reader that the performance aspect of action is a metaphor and it does not mean that politics is an artistic event, but it is merely like a performance because it takes place in a public arena and must be witnessed by others.[23]

Arendt believes that political action is both unpredictable and irreversible. Action is unpredictable because it falls into a web of human relationships and one can never be sure in advance how significant an action will be or how long it will reverberate in the community (*HC* 184). Unlike most philosophical conceptions of freedom that equate freedom with sovereignty, Arendt believes that freedom involves a lack of control, since actors cannot predict the consequences or results of what they do in advance (*HC* 234). The unpredictability of action is not due to a lack of foresight or planning by those who would seek to control politics, because action is inherently unpredictable and unleashes a chain of consequences into a web of human relationships that cannot be entirely constructed in advance. Action is also irreversible, because once the action occurs it cannot be taken back, and it remains with the community for as long as the plurality of citizens continue to discuss and remember it. Action has a staying power that cannot be thoroughly controlled, but is decided by the community into which the action falls.

Arendt claims that the unpredictability and irreversibility of political action can be countered through the ability to make promises and through the power to forgive. The unpredictability of action is remedied by the ability for humans to make and keep promises that somewhat stabilize action. Through promising, an actor can make indications to the community concerning the future, which can provide steadiness. The irreversibility of political action is tempered by the ability for humans to forgive one another and forgive mistakes of the past. One alternative to forgiveness is punishment, which also seeks to make reparations for past actions and put an end to the original transgression (*HC* 241). Both forgiveness and punishment differ from vengeance or revenge that reacts to the original wrong and perpetuates it. Forgiveness offers a provisional ending to any pain caused by action and alleviates its irreversibility.

Overall, Arendt's concept of political action is anti-totalitarian because it prioritizes the differences between persons, instead of crushing human plurality and discouraging individual action. Whereas totalitarianism promotes an atmosphere of fear, paranoia and silence that inhibits persons from objecting to the regime, Arendt's concept of political action encourages and tolerates the differences between persons in an arena of freedom in which persons may speak and act as they wish. Overall, Arendt believes that through action, humans manifest their freedom, which is in contrast to the needs of laboring and the utility of fabrication that are forced upon us.[24] The goal of politics is freedom which contrasts with totalitarian ideologies that seek to preserve the sovereignty of those in power and to promote the ideology of the cause, at the expense of the larger community. For Arendt, the spectators of political action have their say since they determine the meaning of the action for the community through debate and openness. Alternatively, totalitarianism promotes a strongman rule in which the ruler has ultimate power and cannot be questioned. Arendt's view of politics is one in which power exists between persons when they act together in concert and cannot be dictated from above because true power demands free consent. What occurs in repressive regimes are forceful acts achieved through fear that never secure the loyalty of the people beyond the temporary condition of oppression. In Arendt's view, political opinions should be solicited to discover how individuals see the world and to help make decisions that involve the interests of all. In her later works, Arendt will go on to tackle the issue of political judgment, which concerns how the spectators evaluate a particular action and come to a consensus. In contrast to universal politics which claims that there is only one correct political decision, Arendt's theory is open to the possibility of different communities coming to different conclusions about the meaning of action based upon what is right for them.

For Arendt, the presence of flourishing political action in a community is a signal that freedom is thriving. Regrettably, Arendt believes that in the modern age, politics has lost the original sense of political action, in part, because there has been a substitution of making for acting. When Plato, for example, bases politics on the philosopher king who rules according to a theoretical blueprint or pattern of the most just state, Arendt argues that this makes politics similar to the fabrication process since those in power create the object of the political state according to a preconceived plan, just like a master craftsman creates a thing (*HC* 221). Arendt thinks that Plato sought to escape the haphazardness and unpredictability of democracy by basing politics on universal and true ideas, but in doing so, he extinguishes the plurality of the people. Political action becomes an activity that is thought of as a means to a preconceived end based upon the ideas of the few who know the truth, rather than a realm of plurality and discussion that cannot be entirely controlled. Following the Platonic model, universal theory about politics generally construes of politics as a form of predictable making, rather than embracing the unpredictable and irreversible aspects of action. Arendt calls this phenomenon the 'traditional substitution of making for acting', that treats other persons as manageable material of fabrication, as if they were things (*HC* 220). Arendt's view of politics differs because it maintains the importance of diversity within politics and rejects the idea that politics can be fabricated by the few in rule. In some respects, Arendt is heavily influenced by Aristotle, since he maintains the importance of having distinctions between different types of activities. More specifically, Aristotle thought that *poiēsis*, or making, was different from *praxis*, or acting, even though Arendt asserts that Aristotle is also guilty of substituting making for acting, since he describes the statesperson as someone who 'makes', or fabricates the state (*HC* 196).

Ultimately, Arendt denies the standard philosophical position that political theory determines political practice. She asserts that to take the plurality of humanity seriously means

> one has got to modify this notion of the unity of theory and practice to such an extent that it will be unrecognizable for those who have tried their hand at it before. I really believe that you can only act in concert and I really believe that you can only think by yourself.[25]

Thus, politics does not follow a temporality of abstract philosophical thought followed by actualizing it through the imitation of that idea. Fabrication is an inappropriate mode of politics because it reduces persons to material to be organized and manipulated according to an abstract plan that all must agree to even though it represents the *doxai* of a few. Political action, on the other hand, involves the differing views of community members who discuss with one another what is best for the community, rather than seek to control or manipulate it in isolation.

Arendt's overall description of political action has been interpreted in various ways by her readers. Some thinkers focus on the performance aspect of political action in which action is described as being similar to an artistic performance on a stage in front of an audience. Margaret Canovan and Dana Villa, for example, argue that action is a type of performance that differs from labor because it takes place in public and does not focus on socio-economic considerations or the administration of household or work tasks, but reveals persons in their uniqueness.[26] Adriana Cavarero describes the act of speech as being more important than the content of speech in political action. She thinks that what matters most for Arendt is the relationship developed between people and the expression of the self disclosed in action, rather than emphasizing the content of the actual policies. [27] Some argue that Arendt is an elitist since she focuses upon the immortality and excellence of the political actors, while still others hold that her view of politics is democratic since it prioritizes the equal participation of all in the political process.[28] Maurizio Passerin d'Entrèves, Sheyla Benhabib and Jürgen Habermas emphasize the expressive and communicative aspect to Arendt's description of action that seeks consensus through discussion and decision making.[29] While there is a great deal at stake depending upon which aspect of action is emphasized, what is clear is that Arendt thinks that political action is an importantly significant human activity and that it combats totalitarianism by prioritizing plurality. In later years, Arendt stresses that the spectator's role in witnessing the action is even more important than the actor's role, because the spectators determine the significance of that action to the community.

MODERN ALIENATION AND THE SOCIAL

In addition to positively describing the categories of human activity, labor, work and action, a great deal of *The Human Condition* explores Arendt's diagnosis of current politics and the problems that emerge when these categories of activity fail to be distinct from one another. The last section of *The Human Condition* discusses modern alienation and the factors in the modern age that have led to the categorical confusion in human activities.[30] For Arendt, there are three pivotal events that impact the modern age and contribute to world alienation in the West. First, Arendt thinks that with the European 'discovery' of America and the mapping of the globe, the world shrinks, leading to a sense of alienation from the world. The fact of being able to travel to all parts of the world makes the world manageable within the minds of humans and puts a distance between humans and what is immediately before them. The alienation of this process is increased by the technological advance of the airplane, which shrinks the globe further and allows humans to think of themselves as detached from the world, or in abstraction from it. Rather than feeling connected to a sense of place, one can imagine oneself in abstraction from a particular place since it is possible to be on the other side of the globe relatively quickly (*HC* 250–1).

Second, Arendt believes that the Reformation, including the loss of faith, but more importantly, the divestiture of wealth and land owned by the Church, causes an economic instability that leads to the rise of capitalism and significant portions of society being alienated from their place in the world. Arendt thinks that the expropriation of church property in the Reformation causes the downfall of the feudal system. Instead of producing a more equal distribution of wealth, the expropriation of the land ends the limited protection that the system provided for some who had previously been connected to a specific place, through work on private land. Land, which was once economically stable, is turned into more fluid wealth without a sense of more permanent attachment and peasants are turned into laborers and are forced to live 'from hand to mouth' (*HC* 255).[31] According to Patricia Bowen-Moore, when private property becomes a public article for exchange after the expropriation of church lands, then the experience of private and public life becomes compromised, because the stability of the private can no longer be assured.[32] Arendt thinks this brings about the decline of both the public and the private realms because there is no longer a private place for security, or a public space for action (*HC* 251–7). Furthermore, the rise of capitalism leads to the problem of the advancing speed of the accumulation of wealth and promotes mass production and consumption of goods. This results in further world alienation, as the stability of the fabricated world is weakened and no longer provides the durable space against nature. Moreover, capitalism encourages the rise of imperialism, since the focus of society becomes the increased accumulation of goods and wealth which must expand beyond national borders.[33]

Finally, the invention of the telescope leads to scepticism in sense experience, as well as the ability to think of nature from a point of view that is detached from earth, which the philosophical tradition refers to as the Archimedean point of knowledge. Archimedes was an ancient Greek mathematician who believed that a point in the universe could be found upon which one could balance a lever in order to move the earth. The invention of the telescope allows one to think from the point of view of disembodied space or from the 'objectivity' of the Archimedean point, rather than from the point of view of an earthly bound human body. Lisa Jane Disch thinks Arendt rejects philosophizing from an Archimedean point because in its abstract 'objectivity', it mistakenly purports to take place outside of the web of human relationships and plurality.[34] The immediate philosophical response to the invention of the telescope was Descartes' doubt and scepticism concerning all knowledge, signalling a lack of confidence in the senses. Cartesian philosophy drives humanity inward to introspection and promotes a loss of the common sense that normally arises when sharing the world with others. Descartes moves the Archimedean point into the self, to the 'I think', because the existence of the mind was the most certain factor of knowledge according to him, causing humans to escape from the world into the self. The 'I think', or the *cogito*, becomes Descartes' Archimedean point because it is what grounds all knowledge and becomes the point of 'objectivity' for knowledge. All of these events lead to alienation and a feeling of homelessness, or not belonging to either the earth or the fabricated human world. Dana Villa thinks this makes persons of the modern age more susceptible to totalitarian fictions, because of the heightened sense of loneliness, alienation from the world, and the lack of meaningful contact with others.[35] Alternatively, Arendt's theory promotes the possibility of genuine political action that is inspired by 'love for the world', rather than alienation from it (*HC* 324). Elisabeth Young-Bruehl thinks that what Arendt calls *amor mundi*, or love of the world, is the theme that unites all of Arendt's thought. In fact, Arendt's original title for *The Human Condition* was 'Amor Mundi', because her theory of political action stresses attachment to place and to others.[36]

The most important result of world alienation and one of the most urgent political problems of the modern age for Arendt, concerns the overlap of the public and private spheres. Arendt believes that labor in ancient Greek society was an activity that occurs privately. In the privacy of the household, the labor that was necessary to sustain life was kept hidden from public view. Arendt claims that for the Greeks, to be within the household like a servant or slave, meant to be deprived of public life and the private realm was a realm of deprivation. Since the activity of the household was private, one could not distinguish oneself there. In addition, the household was not run according to the equality of all its members like politics, but it was run by the head of the family, or the *paterfamilias*, so the household excluded freedom and equality and the persons within it were enslaved by the necessity of labor (*HC* 32). The privacy of the household did have some positive aspects, particularly in providing a space of protection to shield one from the glare of the public world, but it was decisively different from the political realm. In contrast to the private realm, the public realm is a space that relates and separates people and includes freedom, equality and distinction through words and deeds. The public realm is open to the view of others and encourages public discussion of its events. For Arendt, maintaining the separateness of these spheres preserves the integrity of each realm and makes a thriving politics possible. The separation of these realms provides a private space for security and protection from the public world, as well as a public space for discussing and acting with others.

Arendt's critique of the modern age is that the separateness of the public and the private has been compromised, which Arendt describes as the emergence of the social. Many factors contribute to the blurring of these spheres, but there are indications of the overlap between the public and private as early as the Roman Empire in which the political nature of humanity was mistakenly translated as 'social' by Seneca (*HC* 23). The rise of the nation-state contributed to this problem since it based politics on the model of a family who is taken care of by the administrative bookkeeping of the state, rather than recognizing politics as a realm of freedom and distinction where issues of public concern are discussed (*HC* 28). Society, a strange mix of both public and private characteristics, is guided by conformity, rather than the distinction of political actors. In addition, society tends to promote a community of laborers and job holders, whose primary concern involves the need to sustain human life, rather than focusing on free political activities (*HC* 46). The emergence of society discourages the possibility of political action because the distinction and difference that is so important in the realm of politics gets transferred into the private realm and occurs through intimacy in private relationships (*HC* 41). Arendt believes that there is a mass phenomenon of loneliness and alienation that results from the loss of the public realm. In the quest to satiate private needs, exposure to seeing and hearing others' opinions is limited and humans are deprived of that experience, as well as being divested of the chance for personal immortality displayed in action (*HC* 56, 58). In addition, the limited exposure to others also prevents persons from having an objective relation to reality because there is a loss of contact with other perspectives that are required to confirm the objectivity of the world (*HC* 58). Arendt discusses this aspect of the social as the rise of the idiot, since it concerns an isolated self that is only concerned with his or her own life and necessities, rather than politics.[37] Furthermore, the private realm is also diminished since it loses its sacred character of providing a location of safety and protection from the public world and becomes open to the view of the public, as issues that were once deemed 'private', are openly discussed (*HC* 69). Arendt believes that in totalitarian regimes, there is a complete loss of the separation between the public and the private because the regime tries to dominate all aspects of a person and fails to provide either a public space for action or a private space for protection (*EU* 333). Politically, the social promotes a rule by 'nobody', since individual political action is destroyed and the bureaucracy of government takes over the administration of the tasks of life (*HC* 40).

While the loss of the public realm of action and distinction of the individual is certainly problematic for Arendt, a further concern with the emergence of the social is that politics are more likely to be focused upon private needs, rather than the public good and the sense of what is best for the entire community is lost, turning private matters into an area for public concern (*HC* 69). Political questions begin to involve how to best advance the private needs and interests of specific groups in order to gain even more wealth (*HC* 68). What is lost is the concern for the whole, as well as the expression of a diversity of perspectives needed to make decisions for the whole. With the private and public realms compromised, politics sinks to the level of individual gain, rather than public good. This means that generally, the most powerful and wealthy get their needs addressed, while the impact of these decisions on the broader community is ignored.

The social realm involves the blurring of the public and the private, but also concerns the overlap between the categories of labor and work, at the expense of the most important activity for Arendt: political action. Arendt believes that first work begins to take priority over action. With the rise of industrialization, Arendt thinks there is an emphasis on the life of *homo faber* that turns usefulness and utility into the ultimate standards for life and views the world only in its material aspect to sustain fabrication, losing any other type of significance or meaning (*HC* 158). According to Elizabeth M. Meade, values have degenerated into exchange values for Arendt and this type of language has rendered all other values meaningless.[38] The world of science and technology trumps the importance of speech and action and the result is a type of world alienation in which humans no longer have a fitting place in the world. The invention of nuclear technology is particularly troubling to Arendt, who sees a new capacity for humanity to destroy itself. In addition, the overemphasis of work and fabrication causes work to lose its ability to provide a stable environment against nature because of the rise of consumerism. For Arendt, many fabricated items made through work become more like objects of labor, since they are easily used up, thrown away and replaced rapidly (*HC* 57). She claims that chairs and tables have begun to be used up almost as quickly as food, since style and fashion have increased in importance and the swift turnover of fabricated goods is encouraged (*HC* 124). The precious workmanship present in many works of fabrication is reduced, leading society to consume and devour 'our houses and furniture and cars' as quickly as labor products, as if they would spoil quickly (*HC* 126). Activity in general begins to exclusively concern securing the necessities of life and seeking abundance, so that the main purpose of work, which was to provide stability and permanence, is significantly lessened.

As a result of the rise of consumerism, Arendt thinks that the emphasis on *homo faber* is replaced by elevating labor, or *animal laborans*, to the highest position in the active life. Work becomes like laboring because its demands become cyclical and the products that it makes are much more perishable. If owning property and taking care of private needs is at the centre of life, then freedom and equality that manifests itself in political action also wanes and the only real interest of persons concerns sheer survival and the accumulation of wealth. Free time is spent participating in private hobbies rather than in political activities, resulting in the loss of freedom, reality of the world, durability and permanence (*HC* 118). Arendt also believes that the overemphasis of labor is anti-political since it does not involve togetherness or plurality, but stresses conformity and focuses on the sameness of humanity in terms of biological needs (*HC* 212, 214).

For Arendt, the necessity of preserving the distinction between public and private is central to her work. The invasion of private interest into the realm of politics compromises the objectivity of politics and its concern for the community as a whole. In addition, it puts plurality at risk, as persons no longer try to actively listen to one another's perspectives, since private interests govern the political realm. The rise of the social produces loneliness, alienation, consumerism and a lack of a sense of belonging to this world. Humans are deprived by not speaking with one another and by not witnessing or participating in important political deeds that allow them to distinguish themselves. The most alarming problem is that with the rise of fabrication and technology, the capacity to destroy the world has emerged and politics tends towards totalitarianism, if history and nature are believed to be processes that can be controlled by the powerful. While Arendt admits that the capacity and potential for political action still remains, the appearance of freedom is dwindling and being distorted, resulting in possibly of the modern age ending with the 'most sterile passivity history has ever known' (*HC* 322). The alarming lack of interest in politics is something that Arendt views as a disturbing trend.

Because of Arendt's concern with political plurality, she maintains the separateness of the public and private realms and is concerned about the rise of the social which produces conformity, rather than distinction. Like an aspiring parvenu, the engagement with the social places the emphasis on conformity and apolitical activities and stifles the freedom and equality manifested in political action. However, Arendt's analysis of the social has also received a great amount of criticism and her notion of the social is largely viewed as being untenable.[39] If Arendt's separation between the public and the private is rigid and absolute, it seems unlikely that typical political actions would count as being political, since many of these questions revolve around what Arendt would construe of as 'private' issues. The most blatant example of the problem with the strict separation between public and private is exemplified in Arendt's book *On Revolution* (1963).

In *On Revolution*, Arendt analyses the differences between the French and American Revolutions. According to Arendt, the American Revolution is a success, while the French Revolution is a failure because it degenerates into the Terror. Arendt quotes a witness to the French Revolution, Georg Forster, who claims that the French revolution failed because it resulted in extreme violence and ended up 'devouring its own children' (qtd in *OR* 42). The reason for the success of the American Revolution and the failure of the French Revolution is not due to the difference in the level of violence of the outcome, because the violence of the Terror in France merely displayed a symptom of what was really wrong. For Arendt, the French Revolution was social, while the American Revolution maintained a valuable separation between the private realm and the public good and remained focused upon securing freedom for the people.

According to Arendt, the American Revolution successfully marked a new beginning and attained the goal of freedom for the people because there was more economic abundance in America, than in

France (*OR* 14–17). Since the economic needs were not as acute, the Americans could focus their attention on forming a new government based upon principles. In contrast, the French Revolution occurred amidst the hunger and suffering of the masses, driven by their bodies' needs and the overwhelming urgency of the life process (*OR* 54). Arendt considered the French Revolution to be a stillborn new republic since the citizens were 'under the absolute dictate of their bodies' which made the revolution social, or about private concerns or needs, rather than about securing public freedom (*OR* 54). Arendt claims that the French Revolution was problematically driven by a sense of compassion for the suffering people that caused them to ignore the need to establish principles of government. While Arendt does not deny that poverty existed in America and certainly, the existence of slavery meant that this revolution did not concern the whole of the population, she did believe that the average American laborer was not as miserable as the French laborer, which allowed the American Founding Fathers to concentrate on more 'political' concerns like writing the Constitution (*OR* 63). Arendt claims that the American Revolution sought to establish lasting institutions by advocating the balance of powers and supporting rule by reason, instead of the passions (*OR* 91). The French Revolution, on the other hand, promoted the will of the people, which for Arendt, excludes the plurality inherent in the public exchange of opinions in favour of a rule by the one majority opinion, regardless of whether it is based in the common good of the community (*OR* 71). Arendt thinks it was as if the American Founding Fathers were in a kind of ivory tower in which social questions concerning 'the fearful spectacle of human misery, the haunting voices of abject poverty, never penetrated', allowing them to produce more successful results (*OR* 90). In contrast, the French Revolution involved the private happiness of the people in an effort to cure poverty and secure abundance. Ultimately, the French Revolution concerned negative freedom and a kind of liberation from suffering, instead of the positive freedom involved with political action (*OR* 22). Arendt believes that the attempt to solve social questions through politics is something that 'sends revolutions to their doom' because social concerns cannot be solved through government action and it causes persons to ignore the process of establishing the structures necessary for political freedom to flourish (*OR* 108).

Most critics of Arendt worry that something like the mass poverty and starvation of a people is certainly a political question that can be solved through political solutions, so Arendt is guilty of a kind of elitism by assuming that societies need a certain level of wealth to be concerned with politics at all. Arendt's most notable critic on this issue is Hanna Fenichel Pitkin who published *The Attack of the Blob: Hannah Arendt's Concept of the Social* in 1998. Pitkin thinks that Arendt's description of the phenomena of the social is similar to the gelatinous substance of science-fiction film *Attack of the Blob* because the social is construed of as being like an 'an evil monster from outer space, entirely external to and separate from us . . . intent on debilitating, absorbing, and ultimately destroying us, gobbling up our distinct individuality and turning us into robots that mechanically serve its purposes'.[40] According to Pitkin, since economic issues are by definition 'private', Arendt's schema of politics seems to exclude the poor and laborers from the public sphere.[41] Pitkin also argues elsewhere that Arendt's claims of inclusivity and tolerance are a mirage and particularly, Pitkin sees problems with Arendt's overall description of political action. For Pitkin, Arendt's political actors seem like 'posturing little boys clamoring for attention' by seeking to celebrate the individuality and immortality of their actions, at the expense of issues of social and economic justice.[42] Arendt's problematic view of the social will be further discussed in Chapter five.

In spite of its controversies, *The Human Condition* begins to provide a framework for understanding Arendt's positive theory of politics. The categories of the active life, the importance of political action, the need for the separation of the public and the private and the concern with modern alienation remain as topics of interest in the rest of Arendt's work. Throughout the 1950s and 1970s, Arendt elaborates upon her description of politics in more detail, particularly in response to the Vietnam War, Watergate and the student protests of the 1960s. *The Human Condition* provides a basic outline for positive politics and diagnoses some problems with the modern age, but her next works expand on some of these concepts and seek to resolve questions associated with the important practical political controversies of her time.

CHAPTER THREE

FREEDOM AND PRACTICAL POLITICS

Much of Hannah Arendt's work between *The Human Condition* (1958) and her last work, *The Life of the Mind* (1978), tackled what she thought was missing from the contemporary political scene, including examining the key political categories and distinctions that she thought had been lost from the tradition. Her monographs from this time are *On Revolution* (1963) and *Eichmann in Jerusalem* (1963), but she also published collections containing groups of shorter essays called *Between Past and Future* (1961), *Men in Dark Times* (1968) and *Crises of the Republic* (1972).[1] Many of her essays from this period explore important political concepts such as freedom, power and authority that expand upon her previous political views. In addition, these essays comment on some of the contemporary political debates in her adopted country, the United States. Though Arendt was happy to attain American citizenship and upon her arrival felt that America had a strong sense of freedom and public engagement, several factors including McCarthyism especially, but also anti-intellectualism and the state of education, social conformity, the rise of crime in New York City, and later the Vietnam War and Watergate, caused her to worry about the state of the American Republic, and by 1953, she felt it was 'no longer possible, as it was a few years ago, to stand up for American without any reservations'(*JC* 30, 215). Her commentaries on practical political issues showed how unusual her political views were, considering that they cannot be easily categorized according to party lines. This chapter will fill in the gaps to her political theory, explore her take on the American political scene of the 1960s to 1970s, and show how her thought is not classically liberal or conservative, but shows an internal consistency, given her stress on the importance of political action as the expression of freedom.

FREEDOM

Throughout the entirety of her works, freedom is an important topic for Arendt. In an essay titled 'What is Freedom?' from *Between Past and Future*, Arendt discusses her view of freedom and its significance to her overall theory of politics. Freedom is a crucial category for Arendt because the expression freedom through words and deeds is the meaning of politics. The spontaneity and beginning that is marked by freedom and expressed in political action is the positive sense of freedom that is of primary concern to Arendt. This manifestation of freedom requires communication with other people and sharply contrasts with the inner freedom of will that was the concern of philosophical thinkers like Kant, for example. Many philosophical concepts of freedom describe freedom as primarily an inner phenomenon, resulting, according to Arendt, in the deformation of the idea of political freedom as either a type of freedom from having to participate in politics, or a freedom of the will to achieve specific ends (*BPF* 151–2). Arendt traces the development of the philosophical interpretation of freedom to Christian notions of freedom in the theory of St Paul and St Augustine that, in contrast to Roman or Greek notions of freedom, are not connected to politics, but describe freedom as being synonymous with the freedom of the will and the ability to control oneself (*BPF* 157–60). For Christians, the main concern with freedom is its relation to sin and the self-control needed to combat sinful desires. Arendt thinks that this later influences philosophical notions of freedom, because philosophers describe freedom as occurring in isolation from other people and within the minds of individuals. Philosophers connect freedom with an idea of sovereignty and the ability to make the inner choices of the will manifest in the world. This is in opposition to Arendt's political idea of freedom that renounces sovereignty because political action cannot be controlled and manipulated exclusively by the actor, but relies on the audience of spectators to determine meaning of the act. For Arendt, if people 'wish to be free, it is precisely sovereignty they must renounce', because actions are inherently unpredictable and cannot be fabricated (*BPF* 165). Therefore, freedom exists *between* persons and externally from the individual mind. Arendt thinks that freedom appears in the world when humans act in the presence of others (*BPF* 154).

As complimentary as Arendt was to the American Revolution because it succeeded in establishing a new republic that was concerned with freedom, she does claim that unfortunately, the 'treasure' of the revolution has been lost. This treasure is the pubic freedom of the people.[2] Since American democracy is representational, the problem arises that very few persons actively participate in government and exhibit their freedom, which limits the diversity of opinion displayed in public. Arendt believes that Thomas Jefferson was aware of this dilemma and in his later years, worried that the town meeting structure had not been included in the American Constitution (*OR* 238). The elected American representatives exercise their political freedom, but they are the only ones who enjoy a rich sense of freedom in the United States. Arendt thinks that this means that the only day that the majority of the American public have real political power is on election day, as it is the most significant opportunity to make their views known (*OR* 240). Removing the public space for the exchange of opinions alters politics and government begins to function like an administrator of various tasks, rather than an institution that secures the public discussion of opinions (*OR* 240). According to John F. Sitton, Arendt's problems with representative democracy are twofold. First, he thinks for Arendt, representative democracy encourages the citizen to vote from private concerns without well-informed opinions, since there is no space for average persons to debate issues.[3] Second, Sitton claims that there is no meaningful relationship between the individual and federal matters, which results in the alienation of persons from politics, since they are without a space for active involvement.[4] Sitton goes so far to say that for Arendt, the American Constitution did not just curtail, but *destroyed* the possibility of a positive sense of freedom in the United States because it did not include a local space for public action.[5] Similarly, John McGowan describes Arendt's primary worry with representational democracy is the fact that it infantilizes the citizens by acting as if all the power is vested in the state.[6] Subsequently, the average citizen becomes resentful of politicians, who are seen as privileged, out of touch or even ignorant.[7] Thus, citizens fail to actively participate in politics themselves. For Arendt, failing to incorporate a space for genuine exchange of opinions causes freedom to succumb to the 'lethargy and inattention' of the people who apparently, have not even paid enough attention to realize its loss (*OR* 241). The spirit of the revolution, or public freedom, has been taken for granted and tragically, the American public has failed to notice that it has begun to fade. Consequently, freedom has moved into the private sphere and degenerated into the social. Arendt acknowledges the practical difficulty of mass involvement in politics, as it is physically impossible for everyone to meet in the same building to discuss federal matters, but she thinks that town meetings could serve as a venue where persons could meet in smaller groups, and exchange opinions which would later be shared with the representatives of the federal government. Thomas Jefferson proposed the ward system, in which smaller, local groups, like the counties within a state, could meet to influence political policies (*OR* 257). Similarly, Arendt discusses the council system as a proper forum for the type of political action that she advocates. Arendt thinks that the failure to include town hall meetings into the American Constitution was a very serious omission, declaring it a 'death sentence' for liberty (*OR* 242). The exclusion of the town meetings from the American Constitution ultimately cheated the Americans of their proudest possession: their freedom (*OR* 242).

Similar to the town meeting structure, Arendt often refers to a positive type of government derived from the council system which would be more conducive to producing freedom though the exchange of diverse opinions. For Arendt, the council system is based on organized political clubs and societies, like those that emerged in France after the Revolution and those that developed in the anti-Communist Hungarian Revolution of 1956, even though both of these revolutions failed to produce a lasting and stable government.[8] Arendt describes worker's councils and neighbourhood councils as being similar to the type of councils that she has in mind. In general, Arendt believes that councils are inclusive organizations that tend to spontaneously emerge at times of political crisis and are not controlled by professional revolutionaries or politicians, but are comprised of average citizens (*OR* 266). Arendt does not go into extensive detail concerning how council democracy is meant to work, because she states in an interview in 1970, that persons should refer to the scholars in France and Germany who were already describing council democracy, though she does not mention the names of the particular authors that one should reference (*CR* 232). Arendt thinks that the main goal of the councils is to promote the direct participation of all citizens in politics (*OR* 267). For Arendt, the councils say:

> We want to participate, we want to debate, we want to make our voices heard in public, and we want to have a possibility to determine the political course of our country. Since the country is too

> big for all of us to come together and determine our fate, we need a number of public spaces within it. The booth in which we deposit our ballots is unquestionably too small, for this booth has room for only one. (*CR* 232)

Arendt compares council democracy to people sitting around a table and discussing their opinions to make rational decisions as a group. For Arendt, councils are not organized by specific political parties, but provide an important venue for persons without party affiliation to play a political role (*OR* 267). As Margaret Canovan comments, this differs from traditional versions of freedom that suggest that freedom means taking action on an agenda that has already been set by a particular political party. For Canovan, Arendt's theory of freedom can call 'new possibilities into existence', with the help of other people's opinions and therefore, can devise aspects of the agenda itself.[9] The voting booth is too small to function as a place of full freedom for Arendt, because it fails to provide any direct discussion of the issues and turns politics into an activity of internalized reflection.

Overall, Arendt is suspicious concerning the influence of political parties on politics because in the case of Russia, it discouraged the free of expression of the people (*OR* 269). Even a two-party system, like that of the United States, discourages the opinions of the people by failing to provide a broader forum for discussing opinions. Two-party systems generally lead to interest groups and elites having the most influence in government as they are able to manipulate the electorate by dominating the venues for discussion and framing issues in their own terms (*OR* 272–3, *CR* 233). Ronald Beiner suggests that Arendt is against group-based politics because of the worry that one would judge based upon the pregiven categories of the group, rather than what is best for the whole.[10] The party system also tends to produce an administrative government in which representatives administer to private, economic issues, instead of widespread participation by the people in public concerns (*OR* 276). While the councils, like political parties, similarly contain 'elites' who take leading roles, they are not nominated by the foremost political party members, but are supported from below, and Arendt thinks it is as though the 'elites' almost select themselves by taking an active interest in government though council work (*OR* 283). The councils share power horizontally, rather than most political parties that function with a vertical power structure (*CR* 233). In contrast to views of freedom that proclaim sovereignty, Arendt believes that sovereignty would be alien in the council system because everything depends upon the discussion of issues by the members (*CR* 233). Participating in the councils or in town meetings is not mandatory for Arendt, as she recognizes that the ability to exclude oneself from politics is an important negative freedom and not everyone will be interested in politics. However, everyone should have the *opportunity* to participate and without a public space to allow for it, freedom occurs only in private, rather than public life. Arendt believes the expression of freedom is the purpose of politics and public happiness concerns having the opportunity to be involved in the political process. Arendt claims that the American Founding Fathers were aware of this need and knew that true public happiness consisted in having a share in public life, which could not be satisfied privately (*OR* 115, 124).[11] Clearly, Arendt's views about the council system and the freedom it instantiates arise in contrast to totalitarian thinking which discourages the participation of the people and utilizes terror to make the masses conform. For Arendt, freedom manifests itself in the actions of individuals who discuss their different points of view. The odds of something like a council system emerging in today's world may be slight, but Arendt thinks that it is still possible, though it may require something as drastic as a revolution to occur (*CR* 233).

In *On Revolution,* Arendt discusses the phenomenon of revolution in a positive light. Revolution is the means which may be necessary to secure the public freedom of the people in an oppressive community. The most successful revolution for Arendt was the American Revolution, because it was able to overthrow the government to increase freedom for the citizens, even though it lacked the ward system. The American Revolution marked a new beginning that interrupted the tyranny of colonialism. Yet, despite the fact that this was the most successful attempt at establishing public freedom, Arendt also claims that the lasting outcome of the American Revolution remains somewhat ambiguous because whether the aim of government is the private concern of prosperity, or whether it is public freedom, has not been entirely settled (*OR* 133). The disturbing fact of revolution in general, is that new beginnings occur violently. Arendt downplays the violence of the American Revolution because she thinks it provides a unique example of an establishment of a new government that occurred mainly through common deliberation (*OR* 215). Yet, Arendt states in *On Revolution* that 'Cain slew Abel, and Romulus slew Remus; violence was the beginning and, by the same token, no beginning could be made without using violence, without violating' (*OR* 10). This has caused many scholars to comment upon what Arendt calls one of the problems of 'beginning', or the fact that for the sake of securing freedom, violence may be required (*OR* 13). Overall, Arendt asserts that the violence is always outside of the political realm and in the case of revolution, is prepolitical (*OR* 9). Violence is occasionally necessary so that monarchy, despotism and forms of tyranny can be rejected, but violence remains outside of politics because it lacks speech. Arendt maintains that violence should not be glorified, though it may be necessary for paving the way for the possibility of freedom in revolution (*OR* 10).

POWER AND VIOLENCE

With the rise of student demonstrations in the 1960s, Arendt discusses the political use of violence and its negative role in politics as a suppression of freedom, in contrast to the violence that may be necessary for revolutions aimed at freedom. In general, violence is the opposite of freedom for Arendt since violence is normally used by those in control of government to force and coerce, resulting in the suppression of the freedom of the people. Unlike political action, violence is mute, silences the exchange of opinions and is used as a means to attain certain ends through force. While violence is often used by governments to force certain ends, Arendt believes that ultimately, violence is a very ineffective as a political tool for maintaining sovereign power, because the means can totally overwhelm the end. The use of violence is inherently unpredictable and dangerous because it never guarantees the proper outcome (*CR* 177). Once violence is introduced, pain and suffering spread at levels that cannot be managed or controlled and therefore, any long-term goals that are sought through the use of violence become shaky at best. Arendt underscores the ineffectiveness of violence to achieve political ends by stating that 'the practice of violence, like all action, changes the world, but the most probable change is to a more violent world', signalling the unreliability of violent means (*OR* 177). Arendt thinks that sometimes the forceful use of violence can be successful in achieving very specific short-term goals, but nevertheless, violence is outside of politics because it renders speech, discussion and persuasion impossible.

Arendt disagrees with the conflation of the term 'power' with violence because she believes that power arises in groups through free choice. Arendt notes that it is tempting to think of power in terms of commanding others to obey, but she traces the concept of 'power' to Greek and Roman ideas of power that do not characterize power as a command/obedience relationship (*CR* 139). Tyrannical and despotic governments actually lack power according to Arendt, because power occurs between people who speak and act together in concert and does not concern the sheer brute force necessary to make one's will appear in the world.

In an essay from *Crises of the Republic* called 'On Violence', Arendt distinguishes between power and strength, force, and authority. Arendt thinks that strength concerns a single person, or belongs to an object, and is different from power that concerns people in the plural who work together (*CR* 143). Strength is an independent property of an individual, unlike power which arises among others. Force signifies energy released by a physical reaction or social movement, such as in the 'force' of nature, while authority involves the unquestioned recognition by those who freely choose to obey governmental rule (*CR* 143). Power, in contrast, concerns persons who come together to act, which Arendt believes is the essence of all government as it involves the exchange of opinions and the support and consent of the people. According to Leo J. Penta, power for Arendt is not power over others, but power that arises with others, which he describes as relational power in contrast to unilateral power.[12] Unlike modern and philosophical conceptions of power that see power as an internal property of an agent, power is not held within the agent, but lies between agents when they act together (*CR* 143). Penta notes that when power is mistakenly conceived of as an internal property, it operates according to the categories of work and supports the view that politics can be fabricated. Arendt's view of power is relational, so power arises between agents and cannot be viewed as operating according to technological categories of means/ends.[13]

Though violence is meant to generate power, it is not nearly as politically effective as real power that is achieved through freedom. Arendt notes that a government based solely on violence cannot exist because all governments need a power base of believers to operate (*CR* 149). The use of violence signals the impotence of the rulers who cannot convince the people through regular means of their cause and the emergence of violence indicates that power is in jeopardy (*CR* 153). Arendt describes tyranny as an abortive attempt to substitute violence for power that does not succeed, because the consent of the people cannot be authentically attained through violence. Violence can destroy power through intimidation and fear, but it cannot create it to generate support for a cause (*CR* 155). Terror emerges when all power is destroyed in a political community and the violence never subsides, like in the case of totalitarianism (*CR* 154). Arendt believes that power and violence are opposites because in a state guided by power, violence is absent because it is unnecessary, while in a violent state, power is absent and cannot be generated forcefully (*CR* 155). In fact, Arendt asserts that a decrease in power in a community is an open invitation to violence because leaders mistakenly think that they can retain control through violent means (*CR* 184).

In contrast to the positive gains to be attained through the power of persons acting together, Arendt was sceptical of the militant portion of the student movements of the 1960s, the segments of the black movement that advocated the use of violence, and what she called the New Left which relied upon the philosophies of Franz Fanon and Jean-Paul Sartre that supported the 'political' use of violence to end oppression. Arendt thinks this strategy only serves to destroy power because opponents cannot be legitimately convinced through violence. Violence appears as an effective means to political ends and a legitimate way to interrupt the process of politics, but for Arendt, only action is capable of starting something truly new (*CR* 132–3).

However, this does not mean that Arendt was against all uses of violence. First, as has been already noted, Arendt claims that revolutions often require violence to establish new laws and a new government to secure freedom. If the revolution arises in connection to the cause of freedom with the consent of the citizens, then Arendt thinks that violence may be permissible. Second, Iris Marion Young argues that violence may be justified for Arendt for humanitarian purposes, such as being a useful strategy to end genocide, but it must be sanctioned by the agreement of an international body and cannot be justified in general terms. Young believes that violence for humanitarian purposes must be separately argued for each and every time, thinking carefully about the possible consequences of such action, including having reasons to believe that it will cause more good than harm.[14] By seeking international consent, the use of violence for humanitarian purposes is connected to the power of the people who agree to combat a particular wrong.

Overall, it is clear that Arendt thinks that totalitarian regimes that try to make use of violence for political aims never fully attain the support of the people and actually signify their lack of power. Alternatively, the idea of a council system arises in opposition to the violent methods of totalitarian regimes because the councils are capable of producing power through the discussion of individuals who seek to work together to govern their country. Power is not thought of as something that can be forced through the will of a single individual, but must arise between persons who come to agreement. Totalitarian governments, thus, fail to produce the power of the people because their methods abolish dissenting discussion and their aims are sought through violence. Similarly, Arendt believes the French Revolution failed because the revolutionaries could not distinguish between violence and power and sought to achieve political aims through violence which resulted in the Terror (*OR* 181). If politics allows for free discussion and dissent, then violent methods become unnecessary because the process of politics produces the power of the people who have come to agreement through persuasion. At what point the non-violent protest turns into a sanctioned violent revolution is not discussed by Arendt, but one can assume that a revolution requires much broader support for a new constitution, rather than seeking to alter the outcome of a particular and specific political issue.

In general, Arendt prefers non-violent methods of protest and sees them as an effective way for generating power through speech. However, Arendt's discussion of revolution also shows an acceptance of some forms of violence and seems to promote the unstable change of revolution, so long as it aims at attaining the freedom of all the people. Though open to the political potential of revolution, Arendt was afraid of violent rule and also quite fearful of the lack of stability in government that could lead to further violence. James Miller describes this as a tension in Arendt's politics as a tension between the novelty of political acts and the permanence required to produce a government that secures freedom long term.[15] In *On Revolution*, Arendt not only discusses the importance of revolution and the worry concerning the emergence of violence, but she also stresses the importance of stability in government, if freedom is to be established, preserved and protected.

FOUNDATION, AUTHORITY AND TRADITION

While the emergence of public freedom and the power of the people are crucial to Arendt, she did not think that freedom and power in government were enough for a functioning and stable state. Despite many accounts of Arendt's work being inspired by mostly ancient Greek thought, it is actually ancient Roman political categories that inspire her analysis concerning how to make a republic stable and lasting. Arendt believes that in ancient Rome, there existed an important trinity of religion, tradition and authority that justified and reinforced the political arrangement and provided stability in government. Arendt thinks that if any part of the Roman trinity was rigorously questioned, then the other two aspects were no longer secure, which put the stability and legitimacy of the state into doubt (*BPF* 128). The main factor that threatened to shake the stability of politics in the West for Arendt was the secularization that occurred in European and American politics, because the prior legitimacy of rule based upon divine right was thrown into question by the establishment of the modern nation-state. Arendt is not against the secularization of government, as she was not a practicing religious person, but she recognizes that it implies that new structures of politics are necessary to provide faith in the rule of the people and conviction in the authority of government. Arendt believes that the loss of religion, authority and tradition are not necessarily destructive, but that they disrupt a continuity with the past, making the past fragmented and that these losses require a new method to understand and cope with them (*LM* I, 212).

According to Arendt, the first aspect necessary to secure government after a revolution that contests the divine right of monarchy like the French and American Revolutions, is the need for a convincing act of foundation. In *On Revolution*, Arendt discusses the act of the founding of the Republic of the United States through the vital step of the writing of the Constitution which she believes aimed at securing the authority of the people to rule. The act of foundation is important because with the loss of religion, it helps to provide stability to government and functions in some respects, to fill in the gap opened up by secularization. Margaret Canovan describes the need for a foundation as the need for positive laws to be backed up by some type of higher law in order to be legitimate and what was unique about the American situation was that they went back to a political foundation of the law with the people through mutual consent, rather than to some sort of divine sanction or higher law.[16] For Arendt, 'what saves the act of beginning from its own arbitrariness is that it carries its own principle within itself' that does not need external approval or legitimacy and begins history anew for a nation (*OR* 214). Arendt claims that the foundation for the Romans was political and based upon the legitimacy of the Roman Senate, while for the Americans, the foundation was legal and based on the Constitution (*OR* 200–1).[17] The act of foundation provided a new beginning for American politics that gave the citizens something stable to reference that was acknowledged by the citizens as granting legitimate authority to the people. In France, Arendt claims there was no belief in the legitimate and non-religious based authority of the people in contrast to the divinely sanctioned monarchy they sought to replace and therefore, they failed to create a constitution that retained the authority of the people. The foundation provides a beginning for a new type of political system and so long as the foundation is remembered and respected, the new system can survive.

The foundation of government and the authority of government are related for Arendt, since what the foundation grants is the authority of the government to rule through consent of the people. Arendt discusses the loss of authority in the modern world in an essay from *Between Past and Future*, called 'What is Authority?' In this essay, Arendt claims that authority implies 'an obedience in which men retain their freedom', and it is authority that balances the relation between freedom and the need to obey that is necessary for government to function (*BPF* 106). For Arendt, government with authority presupposes equality and persons who willingly consent to the law without coercion out of respect for it (*BPF* 103). Due mainly to the rise of secularism, Arendt believes that in many respects, the authority of the government, but also the authority of adults in what she calls prepolitical areas like child rearing and education, has been lost (*BPF* 92). Authority is important because it provides a sense of durability, stability and connection to the past, which Arendt describes as being like a 'cornerstone' (*BPF* 95). Without this cornerstone, the ground has begun to shift and Arendt argues that our sense of fitting into this world has been lost (*BPF* 95).

Authority did not always exist in Western government, though Plato and Aristotle tried to establish it with their political theories. First, Plato attempted to establish authority with the philosopher kings, whose authority was granted through their superior knowledge and education. Second, Aristotle tried to establish authority by appealing to the natural difference between the younger and the older, modelling government on the household (*BPF* 105–18). Both theories lacked a true sense of authority because for Arendt, authority requires free consent. It is not until Roman politics that authority, in Arendt's sense, emerges. The Roman Senate was granted authority by means of the citizens who valued the tradition of the ancestors and transmitted this reverence to the senators. Arendt thinks that the Romans created authority through holding the founding of Rome sacred and passing the spiritual and intellectual tradition down throughout the ages. Arendt traces the word 'authority' to the verb *augere*, meaning to augment (*BPF* 121–2). She believes that what authority augmented in the case of the Romans was the sacredness of the foundation and a respect for the precedent set by ancestors. Power and authority were divided in Rome, since the power resided with the people, while the senators retained the authority from the people that was derived from the tradition of the past (*BPF* 122). Once authority was influenced by the Christian era, it became something that existed outside of free politics, as a type of divine right. The Americans modelled their new republic upon Roman and also separated power from authority. The root of American authority lies in the Supreme Court whose justices do not have legislative or executive power, but they have the authority to interpret the Constitution. Arendt believes that authority is necessary for governments to persist and in her own council system she contends that authority would not exist from the top down, but would exist at every level of the state by being endorsed by the people. Arendt thinks that this form of authority would reconcile the problem of politics requiring authority, but would simultaneously maintain equality (*OR* 282).

Unlike the common accusations of liberal political philosophy, Arendt does not associate authority in government with authoritarianism because authority is granted freely and is necessary for a stable government. Modern notions of authority tend to equate authority with authoritarianism and violence, which indicate a forceful and tyrannical type of rule without the free consent of the people. For Arendt, to think of all cases of authority in authoritarian terms is to confuse legitimate power with illegitimate power (*BPF* 97). True authority is impossible to enforce through violence because authority exists outside of those who are in power and must be granted by the choice of the citizens (*BPF* 141). Both foundation and authority are important to Arendt since they produce a government that will last and be somewhat secure, but they also simultaneously permit a space for the expression of freedom. Arendt believes that with secularism in the West, the authority that was grounded in the respect for the past was lost, leading to new problems of humans living together without authority and without trust in sacred sanction of politics (*BPF* 141). Totalitarian regimes take advantage of the modern loss of authority by stepping in when the government's authority is no longer recognized. The failure to maintain authority in government may lead to the loss of freedom altogether and the rise of violent or tyrannical regimes (*BPF* 92).

Foundation and authority are also related to tradition for Arendt. Arendt's ideas concerning the importance of tradition can be derived from her essays in *Between Past and Future* called 'The Crisis in Education', and the 'Crisis in Culture: Its Social and Its Political Significance'. Arendt worries that in contemporary times, there is a common forgetting of the richness of the past, which deprives humanity of the depths of human existence (*BPF* 94). Arendt thinks that problems with the educational system are most acute in the United States because common sense is being thrust aside in educational technique, resulting in the need for colleges to have to deal with students who are not prepared for college courses (*BPF* 178–9). Part of the problem relates to issues of authority, because the authority of teachers is reduced and is replaced by a belief in 'freeing' children from the authority of the adult, out of respect for the independence of the child. Arendt believes this is a mistake, because instead of being protected by adults, who have more knowledge and experience, the force in a child's life comes from the pressure of the tyrannical majority of other children. This social pressure promotes either conformism, or juvenile delinquency, depending upon whether the child succumbs to the group or rebels against it (*BPF* 181–2).[18] In addition, a theory of teaching has developed in which teachers are thought to be capable of teaching any subject, encouraging the 'skill' of learning, instead of stressing the importance of actual and deep knowledge (*BPF* 182). The focus for education has become vocational, rather than intellectual, because it is believed that one can only learn what one has done, and Arendt calls this a substitution of doing for learning (*BPF* 183). Finally, play, instead of effort, has been introduced as the privileged method of learning, which does nothing to prepare the child for the world of adults that requires an attitude prepared for work (*BPF* 183). Not only is this situation the result of a crisis in authority of teachers and parents, but it is also a crisis in tradition, because the past is no longer respected and does not provide a model for living (*BPF* 194). Arendt argues that for the Greek historian Polybius, the purpose of teaching was to let the students know that they were worthy of their ancestors, which makes respect for tradition a central concern of education (*BPF* 194). For Arendt, true education should have a proper respect for the past and prepare children for one day participating in the world and taking responsibility for it. Tradition, along with foundation and authority, provide a stability that is needed for a lasting government, as well as a connection to the common world, and the knowledge necessary to take care of it.

Another important connection to the tradition of the past occurs through culture and art. Arendt believes that art and culture are also in crisis because they have succumbed to mass culture. Arendt claims that the purpose of art and culture is to 'grasp and move the reader or the spectator over the centuries' (*BPF* 203). Instead, society has turned art and culture into social commodities, reflecting social status. Further, art and culture objects have become forms of entertainment to be consumed and used up, rather than preserving a rich and stable connection to the traditions of the past. As a result, Arendt thinks that the masses are alienated because the entertainment products are of low quality and are consumed quickly (*BPF* 199). Though Arendt acknowledges that everyone needs light entertainment or amusement in some form, the danger of mass culture is that it destroys cultural objects by condensing them into easily digestible versions, 'making *Hamlet* as entertaining as *My Fair Lady*'(*BPF* 207). Arendt feels that the 'thread of tradition is broken' and that we are left with the problem of trying to figure out how to preserve the past, without a rich sense of tradition (*BPF* 204). Some may argue that Arendt is too nostalgic for the past and has too much reverence for it, especially since it contains massive political inequalities, but Bonnie Honig points out that even though Arendt thinks that stability and tradition are important, her work also celebrates the disappearance of modern traditional political authority in favour of new forms of political action that belong to the citizens at large.[19] Regardless, Arendt clearly believes that in order for a space for public freedom to be secured and the possibility of political action of the citizens to be realized, there still needs to be a convincing sense of foundation, authority and tradition to ground that new politics and make it lasting. In contrast, totalitarian regimes lack stability, a connection to the past, the authority of the people and certainly fail to manifest the equality and freedom that are of central concern to Arendt. Freedom, power, authority and tradition are key political concepts that supplement Arendt's findings in *The Human Condition* and elaborate upon how political action is meant to function. Throughout the 1960s and 1970s, many of Arendt's essays added to her previous views by directly commenting upon the turbulent political issues occurring in the United States at the time and making significant connections between her theory and contemporary politics.

ARENDT AND PRACTICAL POLITICS

Arendt's commentary on practical political issues show an internal consistency with the rest of her theory, but Arendt's political views are not easily categorized along American party lines, however. Sometimes, Arendt could be described as a political conservative, while at other times Arendt appears to be more liberal. Arendt often voted for democrats, like John F. Kennedy, but she also crossed party lines to support Republican candidates like Nelson Rockefeller.[20] Given the choice between Humphrey and Nixon, she voted without enthusiasm for the democrat Humphrey, but would have voted for Rockefeller if he had gotten the nomination.[21] In general, Arendt distrusts and criticizes the party system, particularly in the 1970 election for American president, since she charged that both parties nominated the person with the most power within the party, rather than the person who had the most appeal, effectively making the voter impotent.[22] Overall, she believes that the party system does not encourage differing points of view, but seeks to have all voters in agreement on issues according to party lines.

When asked directly if she was a conservative or liberal, she answered that she did not know and she claimed that she was not interested in this question because she did not think real political problems could be illuminated by it.[23] Arendt denied that she was a liberal, a positivist or a pragmatist and claimed that she did not belong to any group, other than the Zionists, which she belonged to from 1933–1943 (*PA* 160).[24] Though her parents were socialists and her husband Heinrich Blücher was a communist, she also claimed she was never a socialist or a communist.[25] In *Between Past and Future*, Arendt describes liberalism as being concerned with restoring freedom, while conservatism is focused upon restoring authority, and she felt that both theories had some truth to them (*BPF* 101). However, she thought that both of these political movements were susceptible to totalitarian impulses, because whether one argued for progress or clung to tradition, either position could be used to suppress differences and promote totalitarian thinking (*EU* 282–3). In addition, both the liberal and conservative movements were too close to promoting a teleological theory of history that predicted progress in freedom or doom in the lack of authority, depending upon whether one was liberal or conservative (*BPF* 101). In fact, Arendt claimed that in her classroom, she expected that through the provocative discussion of politics, one student may become a liberal, another, a conservative, and a third something else.[26] Arendt's aversion to party politics and traditional political thinking allowed her to think of each political issue, on its own, without being swayed by the party line, which contributed to the refreshing originality of her thought.

In spite of her rejection of the traditional American political categories, many thinkers have tried to classify Arendt's views along such lines. For example, Agnes Heller contends Arendt was both a liberal and a conservative, since she was revolutionary in one situation and conservative in the next.[27] Alternatively, Margaret Canovan argues that Arendt's thought was somewhat conservative because her project focused on placing limits on natural processes and curtailing human hubris.[28] Arendt's conservatism is certainly reflected in her discussions concerning the loss of authority of government and in education, as well as her strong belief in the need for respect and preservation of the past. Arendt worried about the stability of government and thought that respect for authority and traditions of the past were positive features that should be maintained and conserved in government. In her more conservative mode, Arendt was suspicious of the student protests and Left's appeal to a quasi-Marxist ideology, especially when advocating the use of violence. Overall, she was a critic of Marx and although she recognized that the student protests of the 1960s could resemble a form of political action, she often worried that some of the motives of many of the groups involved were not based on freedom.

In *Crises of the Republic*, Arendt discusses the student protests, and in particular, makes a distinction between civil disobedience, criminal disobedience and conscientious objection. In 'Civil Disobedience', Arendt traces ideas of civil disobedience back to Socrates and Henry David Thoreau. For Socrates, the issue was whether to escape from jail and refuse his death sentence, while for Thoreau, the issue at stake was whether to pay taxes to support the government that tolerated slavery and engaged in a war with Mexico that Thoreau was against. Socrates accepts his sentence and as Arendt notes, never challenges the laws themselves, only the application of the laws by the judges in his case (*CR* 59). Thoreau, on the other hand, protests the injustice of the laws themselves and spends one night in jail for refusing to pay his taxes (*CR* 60). Interestingly, Arendt categorizes both Socrates and Thoreau as conscientious objectors, since their issues involve only themselves as individuals and defer to an appeal to a higher law, or inner conscience, in protest to their situations. Even though Thoreau was the person who initiated the widespread use of the term 'civil disobedience', for Arendt, he does not qualify as a civil disobedient because he makes a case to reject the laws based on individual conscience alone. Conscientious objection is not political for Arendt, since it does not try to persuade others, but occurs primarily within the conscience of an individual person. Civil disobedients, on the other hand, differ from conscientious objectors because they represent a group of persons who have agreed upon a similar political opinion and the strength of their movement is reflected in the number of persons represented in that opinion. Civil disobedience still respects the legitimacy of the laws, such as in the case of the American Civil Rights Movement and does not appeal merely to an inner higher law of conscience, but represents the shared opinion of the group that enters the market-place of ideas (*CR* 68). Civil disobedients presumably differ from group party politics because of their horizontal power structure and the authenticity of their meeting of the minds that does not occur though the prescribed agenda of party politics, but through discussion. Arendt believes that civil disobedients could have an extremely positive role in American politics, especially if they were allowed to work like registered lobbyists in order to include more opinions of the people within American government and could serve to counter the influence of wealth and the traditional lobbyists that disproportionally represent affluent groups (*CR* 101).

Arendt contrasts civil disobedients with criminal disobedients, who defy established authority and seek to disobey the laws (*CR* 76).

Certainly, some of the widespread protest in the 1960s fell in to this camp for Arendt and although she was supportive of groups that worked together to express their political views and sought change while respecting the laws, she was not supportive of attempts to ignore laws entirely, especially in cases of vandalism, destruction of property or violence. In particular, Arendt did not approve of the student protests that led to the takeover of institutions of learning, because for Arendt, it put the educational process at risk. This did not include student protests with specific political missions, like the student protest at Columbia University in 1968 that was concerned with removing an institute for defence and war research from campus. Arendt initially supported this mission because she thought that the campus was a public space that belonged to students, faculty and administrators alike and that the students should have a say concerning the involvement of military research on campus. However, once the students attacked to university itself, the protest was no longer acceptable for Arendt. According to Elisabeth Young-Bruehl, the students had 'combined their legitimate protest against university support for defense research with an illegitimate attack upon the university itself', that lost sight of the goals that they were trying to accomplish.[29]

Arendt was conservative in her educational views because she thought that the authority of the expert teacher should remain unquestioned and that it was a disservice to the students to transform education from focusing on the work of learning, to making education more like play. Controversially, Arendt was also against the integration of minorities that would grant access to persons of colour, regardless of their educational background, to institutions of higher learning. Elisabeth Young-Bruehl asserts that Arendt was opposed to an open admissions policy because she thought the aim of such groups was to lower academic standards.[30] Arendt felt that the influx of students who were not as prepared academically lowered the bar for what counted as a legitimate education, rather than having higher standards for everyone. That said, she did personally support many persons of all backgrounds and races on an individual basis, including children of her friends, acquaintances and her employees, with the funds to go to private school, college or graduate school, although it was done anonymously most of the time.[31]

Though there is a conservative strain in Arendt's respect for authority, tradition and educational views, there were also issues for which she was decidedly more liberal. Arendt was against nuclear proliferation. Arendt recognized the danger of the development of nuclear weapons and other catastrophic weapons and she worried that humans have the capacity to become enslaved by their technological know-how, living 'at the mercy of every gadget which is technically possible, no matter how murderous it is' (*HC* 3). Arendt revisited this topic again and again, warning that with the capacity to kill all organic life on earth, the decision about whether to use technology must be handled in the political, rather than the scientific arena (*HC* 3). Due to her own experience during the war, Arendt was also concerned with statelessness and gave money and support to organizations that helped Spanish Civil War and Algerian refugees.[32] In addition, she supported Soviet dissenters over issues of intellectual freedom and gave money to Amnesty International for such causes. She was adamantly opposed to McCarthyism in the United States, suggesting that it was another form of totalitarian thinking.[33] Furthermore, Arendt's liberalism was displayed in her support for the foundation of a Jewish cultural centre or homeland in Israel and her rejection of the foundation of a formal Jewish state in the region. She thought the formation of the state of Israel was a mistake because it failed to acknowledge and give equal rights to the Arab majority population in the area. That is not to say that she supported Palestinian violence, but she thought there were mistakes made on both sides based upon a 'failure to visualize a close neighbor as a concrete human being' (*JW* 430). Arendt thought that a type of federalism in the region was a better solution, and she argued for a federation of Mediterranean states in the region that would promote Arab and Jewish cooperation.

Finally, in one of the most important debates of her day, Arendt disapproved of the Vietnam War. In 'Lying and Politics' which discusses the outcome of the Pentagon Papers, Arendt blamed the professional problem solvers, members of think tanks and ideologues who supported the war, even in the face of contrary facts. Arendt noted that the American intelligence community, for the most part, had the correct information concerning the war, such as the fact that the 'domino theory' was in error because the only country even potentially close to succumbing to communism was Cambodia. In contrast, the American political 'thinkers' and policy persons were eager to discover the laws of politics and thought they were able to explain and predict political events in isolation from conditions on the ground (*CR* 12). According to Arendt, they ignored facts from the intelligence community in order to preserve the 'image' of the United States and cared more about the public face of the nation, than the suffering in the region. One of the problems was that the thinkers in the American government who were making the decisions were used to translating facts into a language of numbers and percentages (*CR* 18–19). This provided a distance from the misery and suffering inflicted by their decisions and allowed them to decide military matters from a political public relations perspective (*CR* 19). The lying and manipulation of the facts by the policy makers were designed to convince the American public and the Congress of the benefits of the war, but in this case, the lying included the self-deception of the thinkers themselves. The policy makers denied the accuracy of the facts from the secret intelligence community and failed to make decisions that would minimize poor outcomes. Arendt believes that self-deception is extremely dangerous because the self-deceiver loses contact with the real world and ignores facts, causing them to gamble according to calculated risk, which is an improper mode of decision making for a politician (*CR* 37). Clearly, there was a loss of common sense at stake in this self-deception. Arendt thought that what these policy makers failed to realize was that they did not have ultimate control over the situation and they were mistaken in treating their own hypotheses and theories about the spread of communism as if they were facts (*CR* 42). For Arendt, 'the result was that the enemy, poor, abused and suffering, grew stronger, while "the mightiest country" grew weaker with each passing year' (*CR* 43). However, Arendt commended the decision to investigate what happened, which resulted in the production of the Pentagon Papers, because she thought the open examination of mistakes served to restore the reputation of the United States to some degree (*CR* 44).

Though her works cannot be easily labelled along party lines, Arendt's political thought shows an internal consistency. Her more conservative views are connected to her concerns about the need for a stable state and for a meaningful connection to the past. Education provides a basis from which to think about political concerns and includes a proper respect for those who have come before us. All of these factors contrast with totalitarian regimes that promote instability, isolation, and discourage meaningful education that could question the ideology of the movement. Arendt's more liberal views are connected to her interest in political freedom, political action and the need for the people to be able to express their political views without being manipulated by the government or by forms of technological thinking. Again, these views counter the totalitarian position which discourages free action and controls political discussion and the media through propaganda. In general, Arendt was suspicious about party membership, whether liberal or conservative, because there was always the possibility that the agenda of the group would discourage dissent and promote a fascist form of thought.

Interestingly, despite her strong concern for politics and political action, Arendt did not consider herself to be a political actor. Though she was outspoken on many current issues and wrote editorials and articles that brewed controversy, she did not run for office or regularly participate in political activism and often shied away from public life. In fact, Arendt found that teaching five days a week was too much for her because she could not adequately retreat from the glare of the public, and Karl Jaspers noted that the Eichmann controversy was so difficult for her because she preferred to 'avoid the public eye' (*WFW* 236, *JC* 531). According to Elisabeth Young-Bruehl, Arendt did not participate in demonstrations because 'crowds and mass meetings made her uneasy', and she remained a spectator, even though she often supported her students when they protested, so long as she agreed with their cause.[34] Arendt's main work was theoretical and concerned thinking through the issues, rather than acting publically herself. While some may think this is in contradiction to her emphasis of political action, Arendt believed that there was a role not only for the actor, but also for the spectator, as well as the thinker in politics. After years of examining many contemporary political issues, Arendt's research began to focus on the important role of the mind in politics and this led to her last work, *The Life of the Mind.*

CHAPTER FOUR

THE LIFE OF THE MIND AND POLITICAL JUDGMENT

In her last work, *The Life of the Mind* (1978), Arendt takes on topic of the *vita contemplativa*, or the contemplative life, that she had left unexamined in her previous work. Despite her earlier emphasis of the active life, there are various reasons that Arendt was driven towards examining the contemplative life. First, Arendt sought to correct the problem with her book *The Human Condition*, in which she approached the active life from a contemplative perspective, without adequately examining the contemplative life itself.[1] Clearly, the stress of *The Human Condition* was upon the active or the political life, but this investigation occurred in isolation from the mental activity that both analyses the active life and influences how action occurs. Second, and more importantly, the reason that Arendt is driven to discuss the topic of thinking is because of her experience during the Eichmann trial and the phenomena of Eichmann's thoughtlessness, that she called the 'banality of evil'. The reason that Eichmann could unquestioningly follow orders was because he was unreflective concerning the significance of his actions. In the introduction to *The Life of the Mind*, Arendt postulates that the faculty of telling right from wrong may be connected to the absence of thinking and thus, thinking may in fact have a much more significant political role than she previously understood, by helping moral consciousness (*LM* I, 5). In the case of Eichmann, Arendt was struck by his shallowness and his inability to 'trace the uncontestable evil of his deeds to any deeper level of roots or motives' (*LM* I, 4). Eichmann was not stupid, but thoughtless, and Arendt notes that thoughtlessness can arise in even the most intelligent people (*LM* I, 13). It was the witnessing of the absence of thinking and political judgment that motivated

Arendt to examine the relationship between thinking and evil doing, and ultimately, the relation between thinking and politics.

THINKING AND POLITICS

Arendt begins *The Life of the Mind* with the intention of covering her three divisions of the activities of the mind: thinking, willing and judging. The first two volumes of *The Life of the Mind* articulate a detailed history of the phenomena of thinking and willing, how they have been discussed by philosophers over the ages, along with her own views about them. Arendt completed the second volume that covers the will on the day that she died and was unable to complete the third volume on judging, but her lecture courses on the theme suggest that she had a good deal of the theory completed on the topic and gives significant clues to her overall theory of political judgment.

Arendt defines the activity of thinking narrowly, as it does not include all areas of mental activity, or even what the average person would include within the realm of thought. For Arendt, thinking is connected to philosophizing and arises from the need of reason to search for meaning. Thinking is a speculative task that is never fully satisfied because conclusive answers about meaning and the significance of life cannot be fully attained. Thinking speculates about these issues at length and differs from other forms of mental activity that use thought as a means to an end, because it is done for its own sake (*LM* I, 62). Arendt claims that thinking takes place as a soundless dialogue of the 'I' with itself, that occurs through language that is silently expressed in the mind (*LM* I, 75). Arendt often refers to consciousness as being 'two-in-one', underscoring the fact that the mind can have an inner dialogue with itself as it mulls over some intellectual matter. The mind contains an inner plurality for Arendt because it can hold a discussion with itself and thinking involves expressing this inner plurality through the language of contemplation. Her model for someone who engaged in this type of thinking is Socrates, who thought because of his love of ideas, rather than to seek a particular end or answer to his reflections. For Arendt, the figure of Socrates is embodied in the earlier Platonic dialogues that are aporetic and give no conclusive answers to the topic of debate. Failing to make conclusive statements or discover truths, Arendt believes that Socrates merely infected his interlocutors with the perplexity that he felt himself based in philosophical wonder (*LM* I, 172). Questions concerning life's meaning are the proper concern of philosophy and Arendt asserts that one is not fully alive unless one engages in this kind of thinking from time to time (*LM* I, 178). Arendt insists that her own theories arose through thinking and her statements are not conclusive or beyond reproach since thinking cannot attain conclusive truths. Arendt believes that everything that she wrote was tentative and open to further examination.[2]

Arendt contrasts the activity of thinking with the pursuit for truth, which she calls knowing or cognition. Unlike thinking, which is done for its own sake and concerns meaning, knowing or cognition, uses thought as a means to an end to attain factual truths. Arendt believes that thinking and knowing are often confused, as many philosophers suppose they can attain factual and conclusive truths about meaning like those in science, which Arendt calls mistaking the need to think with the urge to know (*LM* I, 61). For Arendt, knowledge aims at truth and concerns what we are compelled to admit to be the case by the nature of our senses and our mind. Truth involves the objective facts of the world (*LM* I, 61). Scientists, who pursue matters of fact, differ from philosophers because the mental activity of knowing facts never fully leaves the world of appearances and continues to maintain a relationship to sense objects. Philosophical thinking is speculative and abstract, whereas knowing concerns concrete truths that can be conclusively attained. Knowing accumulates knowledge and leaves behind tangible truths that can be passed down from generation to generation, but thinking does not accrue such factual truths (*LM* I, 62). Arendt acknowledges that knowing and thinking are not mutually exclusive, as science, for example, can involve thinking about the meaning of the questions it pursues, but knowing must always come back to common sense and the reality of the world (*LM* I, 56). Thinking and knowing are both different from politics, but philosophical thinking is the less political of the two because it is further from the realm of appearances and it does not seek specific practical ends.

According to Arendt, thinking differs from politics in a variety of ways. First, philosophers are different from political actors because they do not seek to distinguish themselves in political activity in order to be remembered, but are fascinated by eternal and abstract truths. For Arendt, the philosopher is motivated by philosophical wonder and asks the question of why there is something rather than nothing, which at its heart, is not a question of practical concern, but a metaphysical question (*LM* I, 145). Second, Arendt believes that thinking differs from politics because it requires a withdrawal from the practical world in order to take place. Philosophy entails a removal from practical concerns and political action, because in order to think, one must abstract from sense experience, generalize particulars, and this results in a kind of homelessness for the thinker who is lost in the abstract world while he or she is thinking (*LM* I, 199). Philosophical thinking contends with abstract universals, while ethics and politics deal with particular instances and situations that are directly connected to the common public realm (*LM* I, 200). The withdrawal involved with thinking is necessary because thinking involves a dialogue that one has with oneself. In order to be able to listen to this dialogue and think, one must remove oneself from the company of others and from the world of appearances to focus attention internally, so that the inner dialogue can be heard (*LM* I, 92).[3] In fact, the thinker can engage in thinking with such intensity that he or she can make the activity of thought seem more real than the realm of appearances and this explains why Plato, for example, considers the abstract truths of the forms to be more relevant or real than what occurs in the world of appearances (*LM* I, 198). The withdrawal from activity in thought is so significant that it is effectively a withdrawal into oneself, a withdrawal from space, and from one's body, which Arendt labels as a 'nowhere' (*LM* I, 199, *LM* II, 11). When one thinks, one is essentially 'nowhere', because one is not engaged with others, with politics, or even with the world of appearances, but has utterly removed oneself to think about abstract ideas.

Temporally speaking, thinking differs from politics because it occurs in what Arendt calls the *nunc stans*, or the 'standing now' which is a time that is between past and future. Arendt appropriates this concept from one of Franz Kafka's parables, which describes the character 'He', who has two antagonists, one from pressing from behind and one from ahead, but this character has the secret hope of being able to jump out of the fight and serve as an umpire over his two antagonists (*LM* I, 202). This parable describes the temporality of thinking because when a person thinks, the past presses from behind and the future approaches from ahead in the battle ground of thought. The person who is thinking stands between them and where they clash into one another from both directions is the present, or the now. For Arendt, political action and willing are future oriented, while political judgment reflects upon past action. Thinking occurs in the gap between past and future, in a standing now, allowing the thinking ego to continually reflect at length upon a certain topic (*LM* I, 208–10). The abstract nature of thinking results in a kind of eternal 'timelessness', from the perspective of the thinking ego, as it can seemingly be lost forever in thought. Since philosophers are so far removed from others and from the world, their mental activities while philosophizing differ greatly from political action that requires others and is future oriented.

Finally, as a consequence of the withdrawing aspect of thought, Arendt believes that professional thinkers, or philosophers, also lack common sense when they are thinking, which separates their activity from politics. Arendt describes common sense as being like a sixth sense that unites the other five senses and attaches them to the world, providing a sense of reality (*LM* I, 51). Common sense is vitally important in politics since it connects people to the practical matters of the world. Arendt asserts that the loss of common sense happens to everyone when they think, but professional thinkers suffer this loss more often, which explains why they so often live life as strangers to the public realm (*LM* I, 53). While the use of common sense concerns practical activities of the world, the philosopher's way of life is solitary, and it is as if they have quit the world of practical affairs (*LM* I, 81). With the loss of common sense, thinkers become distracted from political issues and fail to see the practical urgencies facing the world.

Arendt thinks the relation between philosophy and politics is problematic when the quest for meaning, which is at the heart of philosophy, is misapplied to the political realm, such as in the case of Platonic politics. The solitariness of thinking is one of the most important characteristics of thinking that makes it different from politics. Political action occurs in public with others, where the different *doxai* of the members of a community appear and the community can make judgments about these actions together. In contrast to political action, thinking does not appeal to others' perspectives, but construes theories alone, mimicking an eternal standpoint. With thinking, philosophers seek to imitate the vision of God in order to understand eternal objects, but this practice is ineffective and misguided when applied to political activity because it fails to acknowledge the legitimacy of the different points of view. Interestingly, as has been already noted, Arendt did not consider herself to be a political actor, but a thinker. She states 'I can very well live without doing anything. But I cannot live without trying at least to understand whatever happens.'[4] Arendt saw her quest, and the quest of the thinker, as trying to understand what happens, not trying to dictate or govern what happens.

Although Arendt believes that philosophical thinking and political action are different pursuits, she claims there is still a relationship between the two and thinking can have some indirect political significance. Arendt states that everyone has a need to think and thinking can help an individual reform his or her consciousness. What was shocking about Eichmann was his failure to question his beliefs and his total acceptance of orders. The failure to think altogether is a political problem because it causes persons to 'hold fast to whatever the prescribed rules of conduct may be at a given time in a given society' (*LM* I, 177). Arendt considers Nazi Germany and Stalinist Russia to be cases in which a strong leader introduced a new set of rules for conduct that the unthinking masses accepted without questioning them (*LM* I, 177). Though Arendt does not have a lengthy discussion of the intricacies of moral thinking, she does articulate some views on morality and its connection to thinking. It should be noted that for Arendt, morality differs from politics because morality concerns the single individual, unlike politics, which concerns others and the world (*RJ* 97). Yet, morality is related to politics because inner moral decisions govern the limits to what a person will do, and in this way, affects political action.

Arendt once again points to Socrates, as the model philosopher, who prompted persons to question themselves and their morality through an inner dialogue with themselves. When one is alone, one is able to think and have a dialogue with the self that is like a 'two-in-one', which is significantly connected to moral thought. The self is like a 'two-in-one', and the conscience functions as something that tells persons what not to do, for fear that they will have to live with the perpetrator afterwards and never be friends with themselves again. Arendt thinks that ultimately, what prevents persons from committing murder, for example, is the fact that they would be unable to live with a murderer for the rest of their lives, namely, themselves. Like Socrates, Arendt believes that it is better to suffer wrong than to commit it, precisely because of the need to be friends with the self (*RJ* 100). Thinking, therefore, places limits on what persons will do based upon what they can live with after the fact. Arendt acknowledges that these moral limits will change from place to place and from time to time, which has led scholars to question the validity of her moral thought, but for Arendt, the major problem is not the specificities of moral rules of conduct, but the important problem of when the limits of the conscience are entirely abandoned. When this internal dialogue with the self is silenced, such as in the case of totalitarian regimes that actively discourage individual thought, 'extreme evil is possible' because the conscience fails to set limits (*RJ* 101). In the case of Nazi Germany, the limits that would have been placed by the conscience failed for many people. Significant portions of the population did not think about and judge moral issues deeply. In such cases, Arendt believes persons merely skim the surface of events and are carried away with ideological propaganda, without penetrating to the depths of the situation (*RJ* 101). Part of Socrates' mission, according to Arendt, was to have discussions with people to make sure that they did not contradict themselves and that their 'two-in-one' was in harmony. Alternatively, wicked persons avoid being alone because they are not at home with themselves, and cannot stand the internal dialogue with themselves. For the wicked, it is as though there is an internal war going on within them (*LM* I, 189).

Professional thinkers can have a special political mission in totalitarian regimes because they can avoid being caught up in the political fervour and, for that reason, become conspicuous in the populace (*LM* 192). As political gadflies, philosophers, in the Socratic sense, are noticeable in totalitarian regimes as the ones who will not be swept up and thus, they can be a political force. Under these conditions, thinking can be a subversive precisely because it can critique politics from the outside. Presumably, even someone like Eichmann has the potential to reform his consciousness through thinking more deeply about the meaning of his actions and not relying strictly upon ideological clichés.

Overall, Arendt believes that thinking and politics are separate activities, but thinking can affect politics by having an important role in development of moral consciousness by providing a sounding board from which to question the meaning of political policies in the world. However, thinking does not govern the political realm precisely because it involves a solitary withdrawal from the world of politics and from the opinions of others.

WILLING AND THE PHILOSOPHICAL TRADITION

The second part of *The Life of the Mind*, examines the will and its relation to political action. Arendt struggled with this section, telling a friend that 'the will is not my thing'.[5] Given the numerous references to thinking and judging in some of her earlier works, it is clear that Arendt had more of a grasp thinking and judgment than willing. In spite of her reticence, however, the will is very important to Arendt's overall theory of politics since it is the spring for political action. For Arendt, the will is concerned with future projects and is the site of freedom that creates a person's character (*LM* I, 214–15). Arendt's view contrasts with typical philosophical assessments of politics that place the source of political action in philosophical thinking, instead of, or in a superior position to the will. Philosophers typically stress the importance of political theory and how intellectual theory shapes and influences political practice. Arendt's view of thinking is that it is removed from the world and wills to do nothing, while willing concerns doing something and taking initiative in the world (*LM* II, 37). On the whole, Arendt believes that the will has been neglected and distorted by the philosophical tradition. Therefore, her examination covers the history of philosophical interpretations of the will in order to demonstrate their past failures, in an effort to understand the proper relation between the will and politics.

Interestingly, Arendt claims that the will was unknown to the Greeks and was discovered in the first century of the Christian era (*LM* II, 3). The precursor of the will is Aristotle's *pro-airesis*, which means making the choice between two alternative possibilities (*LM* II, 15). Arendt credits Aristotle with realizing that reason, or the intellect, does not always motivate persons to act, unlike the Platonic view that asserts that to know the good intellectually, is to do the good. While Plato thinks that philosophical thought is the source of political actions in the world, Aristotle realizes that practical reason is different from philosophical speculation, which importantly opens up a limited space for freedom. Yet, for Arendt, Aristotle only allows for deliberation or choice about the means for action, rather than the end of action itself which is determined by the overall aim of happiness from his ethical theory (*LM* II, 57–8, 62). In addition, Aristotle thinks the good actions are motivated by desires that are under the sway of reason, while bad actions concern desires that escape reason's guidance. Therefore, Aristotle can explain misconduct, because one can fail to follow through on what reason dictates, but he does not explain political action in Arendt's sense, because the end of action is the same for all and dictated by reason (*LM* II, 59). Arendt believes that the will is not governed by the intellect, or by mechanistic desires, but freely and spontaneously interrupts typical causal chains and is an expression of individual distinction.

The apostle, Paul, is the true discoverer of the will for Arendt, since he describes the will as more of a faculty for free choice, situated within human beings. However, according to Paul, the will is not friends or partners with itself, but is in conflict, or in a wretched state, because when it wills God's law, the desires of the body are aroused, making it impossible to follow God's law perfectly (*LM* II, 64). For Paul, the main issue at stake is the immortality of the soul, so the will concerns itself with the battle between flesh and spirit, and must try to conquer the desires of the body. Clearly, this focus for the will is not political for Arendt, but concerns inner and private needs, as opposed to concerns of the community. In addition, it problematically proposes that the will's main purpose is for personal salvation and affirming God's laws, instead of doing political actions in the world (*LM* II, 67). The point of the struggle for Paul is to voluntarily submit to God's law in order to be saved, which is an internal and private struggle. Arendt believes Paul's will is impotent because even though it desires to be in union with God's demands, it cannot constantly will God's law and is unavoidably conflicted by the desires of the body that hinder it (*LM* II, 70).

Arendt believes that St Augustine moves the battle for the soul into the will itself, unlike Paul, who perceived of sin as a conflict between the body and soul, rather than a conflict between different parts of the will (*LM* II, 93). For Augustine, the 'two-in-one' of the will is not a dialogue, like the inner plurality of thinking, but concerns the struggle between what is willed and the resistance to that act which is connected to the counter will (*LM* II, 95). Augustine believes that love heals the will and ends its conflict of the will through divine grace. This is in contrast to Arendt's view that the freedom of political action can heal the conflict of the will through the action itself (*LM* II, 101). Augustine's theory of the will is an improvement upon Paul's because the will is the spring of action and relates the mind to the world, except the will does not struggle with politics, but with thinking through the conflicted relationship to sin. Like Paul, Augustine's discussion of the will concerns private salvation, rather than public concerns.

In general, the contingency and freedom of the will becomes a significant problem for Christian and Hebrew philosophers alike, because the phenomena of the human will seems incompatible with God's omniscience. If God knows all that will happen, then how could human freedom exist? In addition, how could God allow the evil that humans commit, especially when he knows in advance that it will occur? This becomes a particular problem for St Thomas Aquinas, whose concern is to reconcile the will and the intellect. Aquinas' answer to the problem of evil is to claim that evil is a privation, or nothingness, in order to deny the reality of evil and God's implication in it. According to Arendt, this results in sacrificing the freedom of the will in order to maintain the omnipotence of God. Aquinas is then forced to explain evil as a type of optical illusion that is created by our inadequate intellect (*LM* II, 34). Freedom is marginalized, since God is the source for all occurrences that will happen.

For Arendt, Duns Scotus, who lived in the Christian Middle ages about a generation after Aquinas, is one of the first thinkers to get aspects of the phenomena of willing right, because he prioritizes the will over the mind and asserts that even God acts contingently (*LM* II, 31). Unlike St Thomas Aquinas, who prioritizes thinking over willing, Duns Scotus makes the will superior to the mind, in part, because the will drives thinking by directing attention towards certain objects (*LM* II, 126). The will is autonomous for Scotus and in a departure from other Christian thinkers, Scotus thinks that the conflict of the will is not solved by God or by faith, but through action itself (*LM* II, 141). Arendt believes that Scotus admirably pays the required price for freedom, which is the contingency of events. Arendt calls this Scotus' quintessential thought because he is the first to take freedom seriously and realize that the will cannot be mastered by the intellect, or predicted (*LM* II, 133). For Arendt, the will is connected to freedom and concerns future projects that are contingent and not causally necessary. The free aspect of the will poses a problem for the thinking ego of philosophy or religion that is not satisfied with the contingency of the universe, but in contrast, yearns for eternal and stable truths. With Duns Scotus, Arendt believes there is the glimmer of a potential for relating the will to political action.

With the modern period, Arendt believes that increasingly, philosophers become more hostile to the freedom associated with the will and the contingency of freedom becomes even more suspect. Arendt argues that philosophers such as Thomas Hobbes and Baruch Spinoza deny freedom and even the existence of the will, because they want to be able to explain causation intellectually. The philosophical solutions during the modern period solve the dilemma by maintaining that while humans may feel subjectively free, they are actually objectively necessitated (*LM* II, 23–4). Suspicions concerning the freedom of the will and the dissatisfaction with the contingency of human affairs later lead to ideas of progress in history that are meant to secure the reasonable and destined actions of humans in the world, instead of making them contingent. G. W. F. Hegel, in particular, tries to solve the problem of the free will through a belief in world history that anticipates the future through the idea of progress. For Arendt, this is a mistake in thinking that denies the freedom of action, by turning the will into an entity that is influenced subconsciously by the destiny of history. Arendt contends that the future ranks higher than the present for thinkers in the nineteenth century, paving the way for the belief in the human manipulation of history and nature asserted in totalitarian regimes (*LM* II, 152). According to Leah Bradshaw, the tradition fails to deal with the will adequately for Arendt because it is either dominated by the contemplative life in antiquity, by spiritual life in the medieval period, or by the philosophy of history in the modern period.[6] Thus, the disregarding of political action throughout the philosophical tradition is connected to the failure to adequately deal with the will.

In the late nineteenth and twentieth centuries, the primary thinkers of the will for Arendt are Friedrich Nietzsche and Martin Heidegger. Though Arendt acknowledges that one might expect a rich notion of the will from Nietzsche, whose philosophy revolves around the will to power, Nietzsche's account of the will also fails. With his doctrine of the eternal recurrence of the same, in which Nietzsche poses a thought experiment that demonstrates the strength of persons based upon their ability to accept and will the same life they have lived over and over again, Nietzsche actually reflects upon the past as if it was entirely a product of one's will and within one's control (*LM* II, 169). This thought experiment eliminates cause and effect and makes the future into something that will have been willed by the actor, or as Leah Bradshaw states, turns freedom into 'gratuitous praise of the world as it is "given"' (*LM* II, 171).[7] This theory of the will contrasts with Arendt's politics because the actor no longer disrupts time through beginning anew and cannot truly cause something new in the world because one must ultimately approve of and accept all events as given. More importantly, Nietzsche construes of all action as being in the control of the actor, rather than falling into an audience of spectators who will decide upon its meaning.

Arendt thinks that initially, Heidegger's early thought was inspired by Nietzsche. Heidegger's construal of the will is a form of the 'will to power' because authenticity involves resolutely facing one's mortality. However, Arendt believes that the later Heidegger who advocates, 'letting beings be', which is a philosophy that urges the acceptance of beings as they are, actually proposes that the will should not will any projects, but merely accept what is. For Arendt, Heidegger's later thought proposes a 'will not to will', and is somewhat hostile to the activity of political willing (*LM* II, 127). Once again, this is opposed to Arendt's views that assert the significance of willing action through freedom in contrast to Heidegger's seemingly apolitical stance that seems to accept what is. Arendt finds both Nietzsche and Heidegger to be nihilistic because the future becomes a negation of the spontaneity of the present, since all that occurs today must be accepted in the future (*LM* II, 143). Both philosophers deny Arendt's theory of the truly new beginnings that humans are capable of achieving through action.

Arendt thinks that the reason for the flaws in the traditional theories of the will is that these theories are proposed by professional thinkers, or philosophers, rather than persons of action (*LM* II, 195). Philosophers and scientists are not pleased with the randomness of freedom and are unwilling to sacrifice the security of knowledge, in order to gain the spontaneity of freedom (*LM* II, 198). Arendt opposes political freedom to philosophical freedom, because political freedom involves others in the public realm, rather than occurring in an abstract and isolated dialogue with the self. While one can be in complete control of the thinking dialogue with the self, one cannot entirely control action that falls into a web of relationships with others. Action engages with a plural community transforming the 'I can' of the will into a 'We'. The 'We' is engaged with the world, rather than being a solitary self of reflection. Arendt ends the section on willing by turning to two foundation myths in order to understand how this 'We' of action is formed in Western thought and how persons come to think of themselves as acting together out of common concern for the community, involving the will to create something new.

Arendt claims that the Hebrew and Roman foundation myths are guiding legends in the foundation of Western civilization that are meant to explain the genesis of the formation of the 'We'. Despite their differences, both myths involve an act of liberation for Arendt (*LM* II, 203). The Hebrew foundation legend involves being liberated from slavery by Moses, while the Roman myth involves Virgil's story of Aeneas and his flight from the burning of Troy. Each legend is told from the perspective of the newly achieved freedom and tries to found a new beginning in opposition to the old. Arendt thinks that in both cases, there is a hiatus between the negative past and the new freedom, or the *novus ordo saeclorum* (the new order of the ages) (*LM* II, 204). Arendt compares this hiatus between the negative past and the new freedom to the gap in time between the American Revolution and the founding of the Constitution. What all these legends have in common is the belief that liberation does not automatically lead to freedom and that an abyss opens up before freedom that cannot be explained by causal necessity (*LM* II, 207). A new beginning emerges without anything that can be traced back causally. Arendt believes that the hiatus points to the problem of the inexplicability of freedom, without committing the mistake of solving it. Unfortunately, the abyss of freedom is uncomfortable and encourages persons to look back to the past to provide some stability to justify the new order in something external to the freedom of humans, like God or history. For Arendt, the Jews look to God and the Romans look to the Greeks to found Rome as a 'new Troy', so that the 'thread of continuity and tradition' is not broken (*LM* II, 212). Similarly, the Americans look to the Romans in their founding of a 'new Rome'. Regrettably, these important foundation legends of Western civilization fail to come to terms with the truly new and, instead, understand the new order of the ages as restatements of the past.

Though humans often prefer to escape their freedom, Arendt follows Augustine in his view that 'the purpose of the creation of man was to make possible a *beginning*' (*LM* II, 217; original emphasis). J. Glenn Gray describes Arendt's problem with the philosophical tradition is that the philosophers were unable to describe the future as an authentic tense.[8] Arendt does not get much further on the issue herself, beyond criticizing the troubles with past formulations of the problem of freedom in philosophy. What is clear is that Arendt believes that the understanding of the novelty of the will has not yet occurred, which means that the freedom inherent in political action has not yet been adequately accessed from the point of view of the mind. Arendt ends the volume on the will, with the hope that political judgment will reveal some insights into the problem of willing, but unfortunately, these insights were never revealed, due to her untimely death.

POLITICAL JUDGMENT

Political judgment has an important role in Arendt's theory of politics because it is the missing piece needed to explain how spectators make decisions concerning the meaning of political action. This is a vital area since Arendt must somehow explain how the differences of opinion, that seem unable to be reconciled in political action, finally take on an agreed upon meaning for the community. Regrettably, Arendt's view is incomplete and somewhat inconclusive because she died before she began writing this last volume of *The Life of the Mind*. The first page of epigrams for this volume on judgment was in her typewriter on the evening that she died of a heart attack on 4 December, 1975.[9] The first epigram is 'the victorious cause pleased the gods, but the defeated one pleases Cato', which is also quoted at the end of the volume of *The Life of the Mind* on thinking (*LM* I, 216). This is a reference to Arendt's view that universal history is not the judge of human's actions, but that the limited spectators are the proper judgers of history and that there is a need to win human dignity back from the 'pseudo-divinity named History of the modern age' (*LM* I, 216). The second epigram is from Goethe's *Faust* which states: 'if I could remove the magic from my path,/ And utterly forget all enchanted spells,/ Nature, I would stand before you as but a man,/ Then it would be worth the effort of being a man'(*KPP* 126). With this selection, Arendt seems to be referencing the need to dispel philosophy of its myths of necessity in history and nature and its denial of freedom and contingency. Arendt seeks to replace these mythic theories with a respect for humans and their capacity to judge. Arendt failed to complete 'Judging', but fortunately, Arendt's lecture notes to courses she gave at The New School for Social Research in 1970s have been published under the title of *Lectures on Kant's Political*

Philosophy (1982) that indicate Arendt's provisional theory of political judgment.[10] In addition, there are further notes on political judgment from a course she gave at the University of Chicago in 1964 that are contained in her archives.

Arendt bases her theory of political judgment on Immanuel Kant's theory of reflective judgment from his book, *Critique of Judgment*. Arendt was fascinated by this book and preferred it over all of Kant's other works (*JC* 318). For Kant, reflective judgment governs the areas of aesthetics and teleology in nature, but the section that was of interest to Arendt concerns judging beauty. In contrast to reflective judgment, Kant defines determinant judgment as 'the ability to think the particular as contained under the universal'.[11] As described in Kant's *Critique of Pure Reason*, determinate judgments begin with universal concepts and subsume the particular experience beneath them in order to produce knowledge. Reflective judgment, on the other hand, concerns particulars, or individual instances, for which there are no universal concepts. According to Kant, with a beautiful object, there is a feeling of pleasure or displeasure, but the experience is unique and cannot be filed under a more general rule. Reflection on the beautiful causes the presence of the pleasurable sensation of the free play of the imagination and the understanding within the mind as it searches for a concept that it will not attain, signalling the status of the object as beautiful. While Kant's theory of reflective judgment does not apply to politics, Arendt appropriates certain features of Kant's theory of judging beauty as a model for political judgment because with it, Arendt finds the tools to retain the uniqueness of a particular political situation, while maintaining a way for a decision to be made within a community. Arendt rejects politics governed by universal rules as tyrannical because this form of politics does not admit legitimate differences in opinions of the citizens. Reflective judgments of taste are a more appropriate model for making political decisions for Arendt because they remain open to legitimate variation of thought and action, without completely abandoning the need to make a judgment.

Arendt believes that it is the spectators, or the audience of the political action, that make political judgments, rather than the political actors who distinguish themselves through their action. Arendt borrows the difference between the actor and spectator from Kant's politics and theory of history. In Kant's political writings on the French Revolution, he looks at the revolution from two different perspectives.

Even though Kant himself is sympathetic with the cause of the French Revolution, he believes that from the perspective of morality, the French Revolution is wrong because a violent revolution cannot be justified ethically. In Kant's ethics, violent rebellion is never justified and those who act for the cause of the revolution are morally culpable. However, from the perspective of history, the revolution is positive because it proves the moral progress of humanity as a species. The spectators feel a sense of enthusiasm because the French Revolution signals that humanity is progressing by rejecting monarchy and moving towards a political community involving individuals who legislate themselves. The difference between the role of the actor and spectator raises questions in Kant's philosophy, since Kant aims at being systematically coherent, which is difficult, given the divergent response to the same event. For Arendt, this distinction is not problematic and actually assists her in being able to articulate the difference in roles between the political actor and the audience of spectators who witness the action. Though Arendt disagrees with the thesis that there is moral progress in history, this Kantian division between the actor and spectator allows her to underscore the idea that the spectators have a different and in her view, better, vantage point from which to judge action.

By emphasizing the role of the spectator, Arendt follows Kant's privilege of taste over genius in the *Critique of Judgment*. Kant thought that taste, which is used to judge an art object, is far more important than the genius and originality needed by the artist who creates the art work.[12] For Kant, the purpose of art was not to fulfil the personality of the creator, but for it to be judged aesthetically by the audience. Similarly, Arendt believes the spectator of a political event is more important than the actor, because without the spectator, there would be no space for the action to take place and no agreed upon meaning attached to it for the community (*KPP* 62–3, 65). In Arendt's earlier work, *The Human Condition*, the actors are seemingly given priority as the ones who distinguish themselves through political activity, but in the later work, the spectators are given a more important role than the actors, because it is the spectators who decide the meaning of a political action by judging it.

In contrast to political action which is future oriented, political judgment occurs retrospectively for Arendt. After the action takes place, it is the spectators who decide what the event means through the use of political judgment.[13] Political judgment is not conclusive and does not create the one and only possible meaning for the act, but rather, is indeterminate and open to different consenting conclusions as time passes. An action that is judged positively at first may later be judged as negative for a community, or vice versa. Arendt believes that it is important that judgments remain open to further determinations and be flexible enough to adapt to the changing political situation. Yet, in spite of the flexibility of political judgment, judgment is not arbitrary for Arendt. The spectators are not personally involved in the action and are meant to occupy an impartial position from which to judge it that will be correct for that community.

Interestingly, Arendt describes the difference between the spectators and the actors, as a difference between theory and practice (*KPP* 61). The spectators who judge take the role of the theoreticians for Arendt, while the actors take the role of the practitioners. It is clear that Arendt's division between the theory and practice is not traditional. Since the spectators do not act, but judge, they fulfil the theory side of the equation, but with two important qualifications. First, judging differs from thinking because it does not leave the world of appearances, unlike abstract philosophical theory. The other and more important difference between Arendt's division of theory and practice and its traditional interpretation is that for Arendt, the judgment about the action does not have any practical consequences for the action itself because the action is already in the past (*KPP* 44). Arendt inverts the traditional philosophical relationship of theory to practice, because theory does not come prior to practice, or rationally ground practice, as it would in a politics based on the fabrication of the state. Judgment is retrospective and does not initiate action in the future.

According to Arendt's lecture notes, it appears that political judgment is a complicated process that begins with the sense of taste of the spectator, which Arendt connects to the oral sensation of taste. Arendt distinguishes the sense of taste along with the sense of smell, from the rest of the senses for two important reasons.[14] First, Arendt claims that the sensations of taste and smell are different from the other senses because they are private and subjective. The other sensations of sight, hearing and touch are more objective because they are easily represented in the mind, capable of being shared with others and can be recalled to memory without difficulty, even when they are no longer present (*KPP* 64). Arendt believes that this is not the case for smell and taste. The smell of a rose, for example, cannot be before the mind in the same way that the melody of a song can be reconstructed if it is absent (*KPP* 66). Taste and smell are sensations that are private and incommunicable and therefore, they are personal and subjective for Arendt. In this way, these sensations are similar to witnessing a political event that is unique because they both lack a universal concept to categorize them.

The second important difference between these two sets of sensations for Arendt is her belief that one cannot withhold a judgment of taste and smell as easily as one can with the experiences of sight, hearing and touch. The pleasure or displeasure that arises through the sensation of taste or smell is much more overwhelming than the pleasure or displeasure arising from the other senses and it cannot be ignored. Smell and taste are more discriminatory than the other senses because they relate to their objects *qua* particular. The sensation of pleasure or displeasure is unmediated by a concept, making these sensations subjective and private, but direct. Therefore, there can be no dispute about being right or wrong about the pleasure or displeasure when it comes to the physical sense of taste or smell and no argument to convince a person that they like oysters, for example, if they do not (*KPP* 66). Similarly, one must assume that for Arendt, the witnessing of a political act causes a direct and unmediated reaction in the audience of spectators that is overwhelming and initially private and incommunicable.

What allows the spectators to judge beyond their mere subjective reaction to a political event is that the faculty of taste is assisted by the imagination. In Kant's universal determinate judgments of knowing, the imagination assists the intellect by transforming sense objects into representations that can be made present, even when the objects themselves are absent, by allowing the intellect to take the lead in categorizing the information under a universal concept (*LM* 85, *KPP* 84). For a reflective judgment, the imagination takes the lead over the intellect in the creation of a representation (*KPP* 84). The imagination overrides the dominance of cognition by preparing the sensation and making it into a representation for which there is no concept, so that it may become an object of reflection. Arendt thinks that without the imagination, political judgment would be impossible because there would be no way to think about the particulars as particulars. The status of these 'representations' is quite unusual. They are quasi-ideas, that represent a particular situation, but without filing the experience under a conclusive universal concept. The process of creating the representation provides an important distancing from the event and is the basis for judging it without bias, yet, it simultaneously maintains a particular relationship to the event. For Arendt, judgments can be impartial because they move beyond private and subjective response, to a more objective representation constructed by the imagination.

The next important aspect to political judgment is reflection upon this representation created by the imagination and the feelings it produces. Once the imagination turns the sensation into a representation without a universal concept, this sensation either pleases or displeases the viewer. But it is not the personal feeling of pleasure or displeasure that determines the meaning of a political event. Reflection *upon* the feelings of pleasure or displeasure that arise from the representation is an additional step. It is the further reflection upon the representation that Arendt considers the actual activity of judgment (*KPP* 68). During the reflection, one must decide to approve or disapprove of the feeling the representation produces (*KPP* 69). One must discern whether to sanction or reject the feelings pleasure or displeasure based upon the *sensus communis*, or the common sense of the community.

Arendt appropriates the idea of *sensus communis* Kant's *Critique of Judgment*. For Kant, taste, or the ability to judge beauty, is a kind of *sensus communis* because it is

> the idea of a sense *shared* [by all of us] i.e., a power to judge that in reflecting takes account (a priori), in our thought, of everyone else's way of presenting [something], in order *as it were* to compare our own judgment with human reason in general and thus escape the illusion that arises from the ease of mistaking subjective and private conditions for objective ones, an illusion that would have a prejudicial influence on our judgment.[15]

Taste, for Kant, is a kind of *sensus communis*, or community sense, because in order to arrive at a judgment of beauty, people must intellectually compare their judgments with the possible judgments of others. This requires an abstraction from the limitations attached to a personal or subjective judgment, in order to envision or imagine the judgments of others. Similarly, Arendt thinks it is possible to consider the reflection on the political action and whether others will agree or disagree with one's assessment of it.

Arendt claims that the criterion for making the choice between approbation and disapprobation in judgment is communicability or publicness. The choice that one must make when reflecting upon a political situation is whether one's position can be communicated to others and made public, so that others can be persuaded by it. The fact that one approves of the pleasure or displeasure of the representation can be debated with others within the community and this process will allow the group of citizens to decide the appropriate judgment for a given situation. Political judgment does not concern merely the *doxai*, or opinions, of the citizens, because one must decide whether one's opinions concerning an action can persuade others. The truth of one's individual *doxa* does not mean that it is true for the community as a whole. Judgment involves deciding upon what the action means to the group, not to the individual.

Like Kant's theory of judgment, Arendt connects the idea of the *sensus communis* to a notion of enlarged mentality. Enlarged mentality, or broadened thought, is the second Kant's three maxims of common sense in the *Critique of Judgment*. For Kant, a person has broadened thought

> if he overrides the private subjective conditions of his judgment, into which so many others are locked, as it were, and reflects on his own judgment from a *universal standpoint* (which he can determine only by transferring himself to the standpoint of others).[16]

Although Arendt credits Kant with the discovery of enlarged mentality, she does not believe that Kant recognizes its moral and political implications (*PA* 556). Political judgments are possible for Arendt because humans are capable of enlarging their mentality through the use of the imagination in order to view a particular political situation from the viewpoints of others. Through imagining, a judge can envision what truth would be like from the perspectives of others by 'visiting' their differing point of view. The standpoint one attains when 'visiting' is a general standpoint of the community, rather than a Kantian universal standpoint that determines the truth about beauty for all times and places. Arendt's judgments apply to a specific community in time, but still retain their accuracy. Arendt's general standpoint comes from the common sense of the community and not from a universal judgment, nor from subjective interests, but lies between them. It is very important for Arendt that enlarged mentality is not based upon one's private interests, which she claims signals a lack of imagination, but that enlarged mentality should reflect the interests of a plurality of others. Arendt believes that the better forms of judgment are less idiosyncratic, occupy more potential positions, and can be communicated well (*KPP* 73). Therefore, the best judgments come from those persons who are able to utilize their imagination to the greatest extent and envision the most potential positions in a community. The community sense is better attained this way and the judgment will be more accurate. This is opposed to the lack of enlarged mentality of someone like Eichmann, who fails to have the ability to imagine the perspectives of others and therefore, fails to judge political situations properly, if at all.

Enlarged thinking, however, is different from sympathizing or empathizing with another's position. Enlarged mentality does not mean that one must blindly adopt another's views (*PA* 556). The point of enlarged mentality is not to exchange one person's views for someone else's, but to envision as many other positions as possible in order to come to the correct decision for the community. If one were to sympathize completely with someone else's position, one would be biased towards that person's situation and political impartiality would be lost. As Alessandro Ferrara notes, judgment, for Arendt, is not about hitting upon the right principle, but it is about including as many of the competing viewpoints as possible.[17] Political decisions cannot be made alone or only from the perspective of one's political affiliations, because without envisioning other persons' situations, a decision would be partial and interested. Arendt asserts that making a judgment based on private interest is a common problem that her politics is meant to remedy. She states:

> Of course, I can refuse to do this and form an opinion that takes only my own interests, or the interests of the group to which I belong, into account; nothing, indeed, is more common even among highly sophisticated people, than the blind obstinacy that becomes manifest in lack of imagination and failure to judge. (*PA* 556)

If one ignores the points of view of others, one fails to judge. Thus, in order to say whether an action pleases or displeases, one must take into account the others within the community.

The final component of Arendt's theory of judgment is the idea of exemplary validity, which is also borrowed from Kant. For Kant, examples are the 'go-carts' of judgments because the particular cannot be thought in and of itself. Reflective judgments are not guided by universal ideas, so in lieu of conceptual rules for a judgment, Arendt believes that examples can provide some clues for judging. According to Arendt, the example singles out an instance that will be relevant for other particular situations. This example reveals 'the generality that otherwise could not be defined' (*KPP* 77). Arendt uses Achilles as an example of an individual who acts courageously and his particular courageousness is a model that can help recognize other instances of courage. The example allows us to 'see in the particular what is valid for more than one case', and the example will help to guide further political judgments (*KPP* 85). While this seems to border on another kind of universalism in which a universal model is used to devise the correct political behaviour, the difference is that the truth of Achilles' courageousness is not the only way to be courageous, but is a helpful example rather than a strict, universal truth that one must imitate. For Arendt, political judgments can provide examples for behaviour that retain their particularity and help us recognize similar acts.

Political judgments are not strictly objective, because they do not claim to be an ultimate truth for all time. They are also not subjective because persons must come together and make judgments with the community sense in mind and not from purely private interest. Through the use of political judgment, Arendt seeks a balance between the need for political agreement and the need for the individual to retain his or her plurality. For Arendt, the validity of a judgment concerns what one can potentially communicate to others with an appeal to the community sense. Since there is a space for debate in politics, an appeal may be made to the community sense which takes the opinions of others into account. One may try to woo or persuade others to convince them about what is right for the community as a whole, but it is what survives the potential or actual test of the community that guides the decision (*KPP* 72). The validity of judgment is not proven, but it is imputed, or presupposed.[18] In *Between Past and Future*, Arendt describes how judgment is meant to function in her view. She states

> The power of judgment rests on a potential agreement with others, and the thinking process which is active in judging something is not, like the thought process of pure reasoning, a dialogue

> between me and myself, but finds itself always and primarily, even if I am quite alone in making up my mind, in an anticipated communication with others with whom I know I must finally come to some agreement. From this potential agreement judgment derives its specific validity. (*BPF* 220)

Arendt's description of political judgment differs from what occurs in tyrannical communities because it involves the common sense, which means that other community members must be consulted in order to attain a real sense of what is happening in the world. Like the way a juror functions in a trial, the impartial judgers must make a decision based upon the common sense of the community and detach themselves from personal idiosyncratic beliefs. Thus, reflective judgment is based on an intersubjective decision that is somewhere between the subjective and the objective. As Ronald Beiner points out, Arendt's concentration on judgment rescues *doxa*, or opinion, from its perversion by Plato.[19] When pitted against universal truth, *doxa* retains a level of dignity that cannot be completely dismissed and is required in the judging process. Unlike Kant's use of the *sensus communis* which remains unchanged by time or culture, Arendt's use of the common sense in political judgment is not capable of deciding what is good for all communities in general. What is considered to be right and wrong for a particular community will change, depending upon which ideas persuade a community at a given time. Yet, a judgment can still be valid for a particular situation based upon its meaning for that specific community.

Arendt's theory of political judgment is dependent upon the possibility for a free space for people to express their views. Arendt claims that her political interpretation of Kant's theory of judgment can explain why Kant believed that freedom of speech and thought were the most important of freedoms (*KPP* 39). Without being able to make one's views public, one cannot test one's use of reason and common sense is lost. Plato's politics is in opposition to Kant's political views on this point, because for Plato, politics occurs within the minds of philosophers and does not need a public test of reason. Political truth is reached through sheer introspection, which involves nothing but what the mind itself has produced and does not consult with others (*HC* 280). This is similar to how Arendt describes Descartes' project, involving the fact that the 'mind is shut off from all realty and "senses" only itself' (*HC* 284). Freedom of speech is important to Arendt because it is difficult to gauge the fittingness of the political judgments without the opportunity to publicly state one's views and try to persuade others.

Some thinkers find problems with Arendt's use of enlarged imagination as well as with her overall theory of judgment. Bhikhu Parekh uses an interesting example in his book *Hannah Arendt and the Search for a New Political Philosophy.* Parekh thinks that it would be entirely possible for a slave-owner to imagine himself in the position of a slave and happily assent to his slavery.[20] Parekh questions the ability of a slave-owner to make a correct judgment when he imagines what being a slave is like from the slaves' perspectives. The slave-owner would see slavery as natural for certain persons and would think that it would be their proper role, if they were born in that position. Therefore, the process of judgment may be limited by the cultural orientation and the historical situation of the given imaginer, making the decision that arises inaccurate because the other perspectives fail to be imagined correctly. It may not be possible for some, or even most people, to obtain a position of complete impartiality and disinterest in order to make a judgment. Nancy Fraser extends the criticism in a different direction by questioning the difficulty of deciding whose perspective gets imagined concerning a particular issue. Arendt does not give criteria to determine whose viewpoint is relevant and whose viewpoint needs to be visited.[21] Imagining all the potential viewpoints on an issue would be an infinite task, so there must be a way of determining the most valid. Although it is clear that Arendt believes that the more perspectives imagined, the better the accuracy of the judgment, she does not explain in detail the practical issues surrounding the procedure, including what to do about persons who may disagree with the impartial judgment of the community, or what happens if consensus cannot be reached.

In spite of the various questions surrounding Arendt's theory of political judgment, Arendt begins to push political theory in a new direction by trying to bridge the difficulty between retaining plurality in a community with the importance of being able to make a definitive judgment about action. She turns to reflective judgment to theorize a different relationship between philosophy and politics that is open to listening to others, rather than intellectually devising universal plans to correct all political ills. Instead of putting politics in the hands of philosophers, her theory asserts that individual political opinions are important and judgment involves engaging with other people instead of withdrawing into contemplation, like thinking. Perhaps if she had lived longer and completed her work, she would have more fully articulated her views, clarified her throry, or altered it in some way to account for any criticisms it has received.

In general, Arendt's overall political theory seeks to combat the tyrannical and totalitarian tendencies of governments based on universal theoretical claims that inhibit the freedom and diversity of political action and make judgments about behaviour in advance, in order to seek to manipulate and control the space of politics. Through examining the origins of totalitarianism and the Eichmann trial, Arendt describes the emergence of new problematic structures of politics that were supplemented by a lack of thought and judgment, which allowed totalitarianism to take hold in the world. Her categories of action and public life in contrast to labor, work and private life are meant to carve out a space for politics that encourages and respects diverse opinions and points of view. Her criticisms of standard political theory as a fabrication of politics contrast with her own views of the unpredictability and irreversibility of political actions. Arendt's politics are based upon a strong sense of freedom that manifests itself in direct participation, but also retains a respect for tradition and history in order to secure the government. Her discussion of thinking, willing and judgment supplement her views of the active life by explaining the life of the mind and its role in politics. However, Arendt's views on a number of topics caused a great deal of controversy. Especially, Arendt's analysis of Adolf Eichmann spurred debate that continued for years after the trial. Now that the significant features of Arendt's theory have been explained, the next chapter explores the most important controversies regarding her ideas.

CHAPTER FIVE

ARENDT'S CRITICS

Hannah Arendt's work has provoked a great deal of controversy among scholars and some of these disputes have played out in the media at large. While there are many areas of Arendt's theory that have aroused debate, this chapter will examine the most important and polarizing of these debates. The main criticisms of Arendt's work include the viability of the separation of the public and private in the social, the worries concerning the lack of universal morality in her politics, the charges of elitism in her description of political action, her controversial relationship with Heidegger and his membership in the Nazi party, her handling of American race issues in her essay on school integration in Little Rock, her complicated relationship with feminist thought and her contentious discussions of Jewish thought, including the complaints concerning her overall method and tone of writing. All of these issues are worthy of further examination in an effort to appreciate why they have inspired such intense and heated debate and to understand how Arendt's theory fails to address many of these concerns.

Interestingly, Arendt would not be in favour of silencing criticism, discussion and disagreement with her work. Arendt maintains that all she ever wrote is tentative and given her theory of political judgment and the priority she placed on plurality and discussion, it is clear that Arendt thinks there was much to be gained through the exchange of opinions and through the process of disagreement with others. To curtail disagreement means to become more tyrannical, and her strong belief is that persons should make up their own minds about politics and presumably, about political theory as well. While it is true that some of these debates over Arendt's work were more aggressive and less fair-minded than her view of how political discussions should take place, the effort to seek to curtail discussion of these issues would also be problematic for Arendt. Generally, I will try to answer some of these concerns by referencing Arendt's texts in search of answers, even though Arendt cannot be entirely defended against many of these criticisms.

THE SOCIAL

One of the most common criticisms of Arendt's work concerns the viability of her public/private distinction. Maintaining the difference between the public and private has been a guiding thematic concern throughout all of Arendt's work. Arendt's worry is that when the public or political realm is guided by private issues, politics no longer concerns what is best for the community but begins to focus on private, individual and economic interests. In addition, politics begins to operate like the administration of a household which does not concern equality and freedom, but merely manages the day-to-day affairs and promotes conformity, rather than distinction. Nevertheless, the ability to rigidly separate the public from the private seems tenuous at best, and Arendt has been criticized on this issue from variety of angles.

One of the main criticisms concerns the content of politics. By rigidly separating the public from the private, it seems that many issues that are typically thought of as 'political', would be excluded from politics and would need to remain in the private realm. A case in point is Arendt's analysis of the French Revolution, which was already discussed in chapter two. The French Revolution is deemed a failure by Arendt because it concerns the social need of hunger, rather than seeking to establish principles to form a new government that promoted freedom. Arendt considers the hunger and poverty exemplified in the French masses to be social rather than political issues, because government cannot adequately solve the private economic misery of the people.[1] One can assume that hunger would be a 'prepolitical' problem for Arendt that needs to be taken care of before one can enter the public realm. However, the widespread hunger of a community seems like a political problem of the first order and that political action should be able to deal with something that is so visceral and necessary for the community. Eli Zaretsky disagrees with Arendt and claims that 'for any oppressed group in modern society, economic issues are fundamental'.[2] Arendt's seeming lack of concern for economic inequality is one of the reasons why she is often thought of as somewhat conservative, as she appears to be against the welfare state because it would confuse private issues with public, political matters. In addition to economic concerns, other issues, like those that occur within the family, would be considered to be private and may also be off the table for Arendtian politics. Issues of inequity between partners in the home, sexism, racism, homophobia and other issues of prejudice, would remain issues of private choice, rather than belong to a meaningful public policy debate, unless they affected public access to necessary institutions. In fact, Arendt thought that certain forms of prejudice were justifiable so long as they remained social, rather than political, such as the ability to vacation with members of one's ethnic group, or to be able to form private clubs based on ethnicity. John McGowan notes that regulating private businesses may also be considered to be social, just as problems of abuse within the family would potentially be private and out of the purview of politics as well.[3] Richard J. Bernstein asserts that the very determination if a problem is public, private or social may be the ultimate question of politics and he claims that Arendt's thought is misleading in suggesting that these distinctions are easily made.[4] In fact, Bernstein thinks that all revolutions are rooted in struggles for *social* liberation from oppression and occur in response to a grave injustice, and he suggests that the claim that the American Revolution was political, rather than social, is questionable.[5]

Margaret Canovan was one of the first scholars to see problems with Arendt's concept of the social. Canovan initially argues that Arendt's theorizing of the social involves two strands of meaning that are separate and seemingly incompatible.[6] First, the social for Arendt concerns the private and biological realm based on the household of ancient Greece, which moves the focus away from political issues to biological needs and necessities and promotes laboring as the most important activity, which of course, Arendt rejects. The second strand for Canovan is the connection between society and high society which through fashions and social pressures, promote conformity over the distinction expressed in freedom. Canovan believes that Arendt has not explained how these entangled strands of thought work together, since blame is pinpointed for the social at both the laboring classes and high society at the same time. For example, Arendt regards the laboring classes as ones who are problematically social during the French Revolution because the laborers focused on biological needs rather than the 'higher' concerns of freedom that could only be understood by persons who were free from labor. In other circumstances, Arendt seems to suggest that the problem occurs when people seek to join high society because it promotes conformity and mass society.[7] This tension in Arendt's work remains unresolved. In Canovan's later work, she asserts that it may be better to understand 'society' as a contrasting concept with totalitarianism, so that society ultimately refers to the 'herdlike uniformity' that could govern both the economic and cultural realms and explain why all class levels of society could be susceptible to it in different ways.[8]

Hannah Pitkin's *Attack of the Blob: Hannah Arendt's Concept of the Social* is the most famous analysis of Arendt's concept of the social and Pitkin discusses Arendt's category of the social by showing multiple conceptual ambiguities with the category of the social itself. Pitkin likens Arendt's category of the social to the blob from the 1950's horror film. For Pitkin, Arendt uses pejorative terminology that suggests that the social 'devours' people, as if the social is an entity, like the blob, with a mind and intentions that threatens massification and conformity.[9] Pitkin notes that Arendt never offers a proper definition of the social, but that scholarship on Arendt's notion of the social tends to focus on either economics and Arendt's rejection of communism and possibly the welfare state, or Arendt's worry concerning the normalization and conformity introduced by the social, or some combination of the two.[10] Pitkin favours the view that the social seems to represent a collective of people who fail to acknowledge the large scale consequences of their actions, linking the social to the failure of political action to emerge.[11] For Pitkin, Arendt's concern with the social is that it threatens the individuality and spontaneity of action, which is connected to the growing technological power of modernity juxtaposed with the increasing political powerlessness.[12] But Pitkin notes an ambiguity for Arendt on this point, because if one focuses on the individuality inherent in action, the content of the action does not seem to matter and the problem with the social is its tendency to homogenize behaviour. Yet, if one focuses on spontaneity in action, then the problem with the social concerns the political impotence it seems to promote among the masses.[13] In addition, if politics concerns free actions whose consequences are boundless and cannot be anticipated in advance by the agent, how could something seemingly external, like the 'social', interfere, and how could individuals be responsible for uncontrollable consequences at all?

Is the 'blob' of society a group of accountable human beings who make decisions, or is it some other kind of external agent that dooms collectives to failure, as in the case of the French Revolution? Despite Arendt's awkwardness in explaining the social, Pitkin believes a problem like the social may be possible, and it is worth exploring and articulating further, rather than dismissing Arendt out of hand.[14]

Arendt was asked directly about the difference between the political and the social by her friend, Mary McCarthy, at a conference in 1972. Arendt asserted that what counts as public issues change historically, but that it is still possible to distinguish the difference between the political and the social in current politics.[15] For Arendt, what counts as public and political are those issues that are debatable and cannot be solved with certainty, unlike administrative issues that can be conclusively settled.[16] Arendt also provided some examples of instances that were properly political: town hall meetings concerning the location of a bridge, juries as they reflect on a case, and the issue of public housing. Arendt thinks that the question of whether adequate housing demands integration is a political question.[17] However, Arendt maintains that the factual need of adequate housing is a social question, because there is nothing to debate about it. In fact, Arendt claimed that seemingly social issues that handle 'private' concerns such as education, health or urban problems have a political side to them, suggesting that the distinctions between the public, private and social are not as clear cut as they appear in her writing and may, in fact, involve overlapping. While these examples do not elucidate the intricacies of what specifically is political and what is social for Arendt, they do point to the idea that political questions are publicly debatable, while social issues are not subject to debate and perhaps are issues of either an obvious nature, as in the case of adequate housing, or issues of private preference which are not suited for debate. Unfortunately, this does not clear up the matter, but it does indicate that Arendt thinks this distinction is coherent and can be applied to current political situations.

MORALITY

Arendt's theory of politics and political judgment has also been criticized on the grounds that it is not based upon objective and universal truth and therefore, seems to promote moral relativism, or the view that every kind of morality is permissible since there are no ultimate truths concerning right or wrong. Most notably, George Kateb argues that Arendt's view severs politics from morality. Kateb claims that Arendt leaves political judgment as the only defence against immoral political action, and he finds judgment based upon a community sense to be too frail to protect society from the arbitrary immoral action of the political actor, or the immoral judgment of a political community.[18] For Kateb, a community sense that varies in time and place is no standard for forming universal political judgments and he thinks that Arendt is wrong to deny the validity of universal moral judgments that hold for all human beings. Arendt's theory of political action that prioritizes promising and forgiving does not, according to Kateb, 'form a barrier to atrocity' and may open the door to totalitarian politics unwittingly, since the content of political action could be completely immoral and devoid of concerns for justice.[19]

Interestingly, Arendt has a few essays in which she discusses the role of ethics in contrast to her view of political judgment that is decided upon by the community sense. Arendt maintains a difference between ethics and politics and most of her work concerns political, rather than moral, theory. Politics is public and concerns debate with others, while morality is solitary and involves an inner examination of the self in thought, particularly, concerning the question of the type of person one chooses to be.[20] As was discussed in the last chapter, the conscience arises when persons must decide if they can be 'friends' with themselves after a particular action. Arendt admits that in her early academic days in Germany, there was a trend within philosophy to ignore thorough discussion of ethical issues. Arendt claims that prior to Second World War, the European philosophical community was not very interested in ethical issues, largely because it was thought that the average person knows the difference between right and wrong, and these questions did not need further investigation. Arendt states that it was assumed that 'moral conduct is a matter of course', and did not really merit large-scale debate (*RJ* 22). However, the moral disintegration that occurred in Germany and the rest of Europe during the war became Arendt's intellectual focus because of the need to come to terms with what happened, or what she labels, the 'unmastered past', that could not be understood by preconceived rules or norms and transcended traditional moral categories (*RJ* 23). An important key for Arendt that impacted morality was political judgment, or the ability to understand new situations without standards, rather than to unreflectively adopt a newly provided set of norms by a totalitarian regime. Arendt uses a metaphor to describe the loss of a framework for considering moral questions which she calls 'thinking without a banister'.[21] Stairwell banisters support persons as they go up and down stairs, but Arendt believes that in modernity, we have lost the banister of moral thought to guide us. Without a banister, one cannot fall back on preconceived notions for support. One must invent new ways of understanding the world that are less passive and more actively engaged. Arendt's description of morality is not based on universal moral rules that are applied to the particular case, because what was crucial for Arendt is that one be able to judge new scenarios with new criteria and not merely accept universal rules as customs. Particular instances can assist in this assessment because they can provide examples to guide moral thought, but relying on normative universal rules may lead to the possibility of them being swapped for different and completely immoral rules.

In 'Some Questions of Moral Philosophy', Arendt makes a distinction between bad actions that can be forgiven or punished that are commonplace and those that should never have happened at all, like the Holocaust. Arendt calls the more serious crimes 'stumbling blocks', and claims that they are crimes that are unforgivable. The source of these crimes is a flaw in moral consciousness, or the 'unwillingness or inability to choose one's examples and one's company', within the self (*RJ* 146). This failing can produce stumbling blocks that humans cannot correct because they are not caused by understandable motives or desires, but exemplify the banality of evil (*RJ* 146). As far as preventing immoral action is concerned, Arendt claims that the best that one can do if someone actively chooses the pirate, Bluebeard, as a moral example and chooses the company of a self modelled after Bluebeard is to 'make sure he never comes near us' (*RJ* 146). The truly criminal, like Bluebeard, are presumably not a difficult issue for Arendt because one can assume that these persons are rare and can be identified and jailed, if necessary. It is the unthinking masses that are the greatest threat to morality, or the ones who welcome any company for the self at all (*RJ* 146). Arendt states that indifference is the greatest danger and the tendency to not want to judge in any way can lead to the massive failures of morality like what occurred in Germany and Russia (*RJ* 146). For Arendt, 'the true opposite of good is not evil or crime . . . [but] mere indifference' (*RLC* 278).[22]

Arendt's limited discussion of morality will not satisfy the moral universalist who believes that morality is based on universal theories of right and wrong that need to be enacted in the world. For Arendt, what is crucial for morality is that individuals think about what type of person they can live with and act accordingly. Unfortunately, this may presume too much of an optimistic picture of human nature, as it assumes that most persons are not immoralists and they will not be able to live with the consequences of being in the company of themselves after they have committed such depraved acts. Politically, Margaret Canovan sees a similar romanticism in Arendt's idea of humanity and in her confidence in the ability of the people to make political decisions, since Arendt trusts in the decision of the people far more than in the views of professional politicians.[23] In 1972, Arendt admitted the possibility that there may be a utopian element in her thought, though she was not intentionally aware of it and she wanted to give the issue more thought.[24] In general, Arendt criticizes utopian theories that propose a particular end to history or politics or that seek to 'anticipate the future in all its details', and claims that this is something that genuine political thought avoids (*JW* 190). The type of utopianism that her theory would be susceptible to concerns the optimistic assessment of the moral natures of humanity, as well as the hopeful desire for the re-emergence of the pristine categories of the political versus the social, rather than a kind of utopianism that envisions some predetermined end to history.[25] Nevertheless, her confidence in the private inner dialogue of morality to usually choose the correct moral option may be too optimistic.

ELITISM

Because Arendt privileges a notion of political action that has its roots in ancient Greek and Roman thought, many scholars have worried about the possibility of elitism in Arendt's model of politics. Even though Arendt states that equality is necessary for politics, some worry that the political actor in antiquity is largely indebted to the women and slaves that made their freedom to engage in politics possible and that Arendt's contemporary political actor might be similarly indebted to the lower laboring classes. In addition, since the political actor is seen as one who excels and distinguishes oneself through action, it seems that only truly superior individuals are the correct participators in politics, suggesting an elitist strain in her thought that privileges the talented few above the rest of the citizens.

For example, Hauke Brunkhorst reads Arendt as actually having two notions of freedom: an egalitarian version based in Augustine's Christian thought and a problematically elitist version derived from Greek and Roman thought.[26] For Brunkhorst, Arendt relies too heavily upon Greek and Roman versions of politics that may unintentionally include an elitist concept of freedom in which persons of distinction and social standing are the only ones who are able to participate politically. Brunkhorst argues that these two versions of freedom are incompatible and that one must be sceptical about Arendt's criticisms of politics and interests in social justice, since her view is strongly connected to an interpretation of freedom that did not allow for equality among all persons.[27] Similarly, Margaret Canovan, among others, sees a tension between Arendt's political theory that prioritizes the excellence of the political actor and the inclusivity demanded by democratic ideals.[28] For Canovan, Arendt's criticisms of mass democracy mean that even though the masses are allowed to participate in government, it does not mean that they comprehend what is the common good of the people, so majority rule is not what Arendt has in mind concerning political judgment.[29] John McGowan wonders what the process for gaining the attention of others in political action is like and whether it is a polite sharing of the public space, a heated competition, or whether there will be persons who are excluded from the stage because they are not qualified.[30] The charge of elitism in Arendt's thought is epitomized in Hannah Pitkin's worry that political action for Arendt concerns 'posturing little boys clamoring for attention ("Look at me! I'm the greatest!" "No, look at *me*!")'.[31] Pitkin asserts that Arendt's politics leave out the vast majority of people and ignore issues of justice. In Pitkin's view, Arendt's politics is a juvenile display of uniqueness, rather than involving an examination of serious community concerns.

There is no doubt, that Arendt failed to clarify this issue by not stressing the need for equality enough and by not explaining how her theory actually differs significantly from the politics of the Greek *polis*. Unfortunately, Arendt's statements concerning the equality needed for freedom are rarely emphasized by her. In addition, the fact that economic inequality seems to be social, rather than political, is a troubling concern. Arendt seems to suggest that either a certain level of economic achievement is necessary for politics at all, or that those who are worried about private economic concerns need to check their personal and private concerns at the door in order to work for political structures that guarantee freedom. These questions reiterate the need for clarification concerning the economically and socially disadvantaged in Arendt's theory.

However, there are clues to Arendt's response to the charge of elitism in her overall view of political engagement. First, there are essays in which she asserts that equality is necessary for politics and that the Greek model of the polis unfairly took advantage of the non-citizens in order to free the elites from the necessities of labor, which she calls exploitation (*PA* 172). Given Arendt's theory of politics, one may wonder how this exploitation could be avoided, since the thriving of political action requires that laboring needs to be taken care of as a precondition to entering politics. However, Arendt claims that the way in which more persons could be freed from labor in order to participate in politics is through advances in technology, rather than further oppression of persons, so she is not advocating that the political realm be made possible through the labor of those who are unable to participate (*PA* 171). Also, Arendt believes that freedom is not possible without equality, and this is why she is against a model of politics based upon household relations of the Greek *polis* which did not function according to equality. Further, Arendt describes her view of politics as coming from the bottom up and involves horizontally shared power, rather than from the top down, involving vertical and hierarchical power. This indicates an interest in participatory forms of government that come from the people, rather than just from social elites. Finally, Arendt's discussions of the councils as the proper place for participation in politics indicate that politics is not elitist in the traditional sense, but open to all.[32] Yet, in spite of these references to freedom and equality, the concept of equality needs to be further explained in Arendt's theory, particularly in reference to the issues concerning the politics of the economically and socially disadvantaged.

HEIDEGGER

Martin Heidegger's name is often brought up in connection to Hannah Arendt's thought. The relationship between Hannah Arendt and Martin Heidegger is a complex one. He was her teacher at Marburg and clearly was an intellectual influence on her thought. Particularly, her dissertation work on St Augustine relies heavily upon Heidegger's view of temporality and applies it to Augustine's work, though it also criticizes the solitariness of authentic life as described by both Augustine and Heidegger. Lewis P. Hinchman and Sandra K. Hinchman argue that Heidegger's thought had a pervasive influence on Arendt's work, especially methodologically, in her distinctions between concepts, her assessment of language, but also in her view of 'action' as a type of self-revelation, though they additionally contend that she has her differences with Heidegger's thought as well.[33] What further complicates the Heidegger influence is that Arendt and Heidegger had a secret love affair while she was his student, yet, during the war, Heidegger joined the Nazi party and became Rector at Freiburg University, which involved enforcing antisemitic policies. He resigned from the rectorship a year later, but retained his membership in the National Socialist Party until the end of the war. After the war, Heidegger was prevented from teaching for over four years, due to his affiliation with the Nazi party. Since Arendt was a Jew who emigrated to escape Nazi Germany, her renewed friendship with Heidegger in 1950 is an issue of ethical concern for some scholars. Connected to this concern are additional worries that Arendt was too sympathetic to Heidegger and forgave him too easily for the fact that he joined the Nazi party.

While Heidegger's ideas haunt many of Arendt's written works, his name is rarely mentioned. There is an essay called 'What is Existential Philosophy', published in German in 1948, that is one of the few instances in which Arendt directly comments on Heidegger's work. In this essay, Arendt criticizes Heidegger for having a concept of the self in solitude that is the opposite of how humans actually exist with other people, and she complains that he prioritizes the philosophical life as the highest form of human activity (*EU* 178, 181). She also suggests that Heidegger's description of authenticity as being-towards-death, or the acknowledgement of one's mortality, is a selfish and self-centred attitude (*EU* 181). This article also includes a footnote reminding the reader of Heidegger's membership in the Nazi party, as well as his poor treatment of his Jewish mentor, Edmund Husserl (*EU* 187). Other instances in which Heidegger's name is mentioned include a book review she published in 1946, in which she blames Heidegger for making Nazism respectable among the intellectual community and claims that his 'enthusiasm for the Third Reich was matched only by his glaring ignorance of what he was talking about' (*EU* 202). As was discussed in the previous chapter, she also criticizes Heidegger in *The Life of the Mind* for his 'will not to will', in contrast to her own concept of political action that begins something new.

In 'Heidegger at Eighty', which was written as a tribute to Heidegger on his eightieth birthday, Arendt comments on Heidegger's early lecturing fame and calls him a 'hidden king' who reigns in the realm of thought, who introduced new paths of thinking.[34] She then discusses thinking in general and makes comparisons between Heidegger and the speechless, solitary wonder of philosophy that was discussed by Plato. Arendt also mentions the story about Thales falling into the well, suggesting the political problem of philosophers is that they are lost in thought and that it is dangerous for philosophers to take on political affairs.[35] Further comparing Heidegger to Plato, she suggests that they both succumbed to the temptation of engaging with politics from a philosophical perspective, resulting in tyranny.[36] She claims that whereas Plato turned to tyrants, Heidegger turned to Führers. She also asserts that she finds something perfect in Heidegger's work, but claims that everything perfect falls back to the ground, suggesting that like Plato's forms, Heidegger's abstract ideas must fall back upon the imperfect earth and cannot be sustained politically. The overall tone of the piece suggests that Arendt can compliment Heidegger on his ability to think philosophically, but not on how this attitude relates to politics. In a letter to Mary McCarthy, Arendt states that she thought there was the possibility that Heidegger was offended by this article (*BF* 248).

The main source of contention in this controversy surrounding Arendt's relationship to Heidegger comes from Arendt's essay 'Heidegger at Eighty'. Richard J. Bernstein argues that Arendt's blindness to Heidegger's error in supporting the Nazi party puts her main essay concerning morality, 'Thinking and Moral Considerations', into question, since it was written during the same year.[37] Stephen J. Whitfield asserts that by calling Heidegger's thought 'perfect', Arendt evades the moral problems connected to Heidegger's work.[38] Whitfield argues that in her tribute to Heidegger on his birthday, Arendt gives Heidegger three defences for his 'error' in joining the National Socialist Party. First, Arendt comments in a footnote that Heidegger and other intellectuals failed to read *Mein Kampf* and, therefore, were unaware of Hitler's full intentions.[39] Second, Whitfield claims that she vindicates Heidegger by comparing him to the famous philosopher, Plato, who was also tempted by tyrannical thought, and third, that Arendt defends Heidegger by stating that he corrected his 'error' more quickly than other intellectuals.[40] Elżbieta Ettinger's controversial book about Arendt and Heidegger's affair claims that Arendt 'went to extraordinary pains to minimize and justify Heidegger's contribution to and support of the Third Reich'.[41] Furthermore, Richard Wohlin sees Heideggerian thought problematically infiltrating Arendt's political theory in a negative manner. For Wohlin, Arendt inherited an aestheticized politics in which the ends of politics are unimportant, and what matters is the artistic expression and authenticity of the political actor.[42] Since Heidegger's *Being and Time* celebrates the need for authentic life and actually seems to scorn being with other people as potentially inauthentic, and since Heidegger did in fact join the Nazi party, the worry is that any inheritance of Heideggerian categories is potentially undemocratic and sympathetic with fascism. Wohlin believes that Arendt's thought 'offers us a parallel, if slightly left-leaning, version of Heideggerian revolutionary vitalism', persevering the notion of the importance of authentic leader types and inadvertently supporting totalitarian ideology.[43]

In contrast to this view, other scholars suggest that Arendt's philosophy arises in direct opposition to Heidegger's thought and that other intellectuals, like Karl Jaspers, for example, are much more influential upon her. Jacques Taminiaux asserts that Arendt's most philosophical works, *The Human Condition* and *The Life of the Mind*, 'reveal at every page not at all a dependency upon Heidegger, but rather, a constant, and increasingly ironic, debate with him'.[44] Taminiaux believes that Arendt's criticisms and scepticism concerning the professional thinker's lack of attention to politics are not only aimed at Plato, but specifically target Heidegger as well. Similarly, Dana Villa contends that Arendt is not an unthinking disciple of Heidegger, but a critic of his thought.[45] While Villa admits that there are some areas of Heidegger's thought that influence her findings in *The Human Condition*, the great difference between their views is that the public and political realm is authentic for Arendt, in contrast to Heidegger's view that stresses the solitariness needed for authenticity.[46] One of the most important disagreements with Heidegger's theory is Arendt's concept of 'natality', which is an assault upon Heidegger's notion of authentic life involving being-towards-death. Arendt never directly names Heidegger, but in a lecture in 1964, Arendt states:

> The life span itself, running toward death would inevitably carry everything human to ruin and destruction. Action, with all its uncertainties, is like an ever present reminder that men, though they must die, are not born in order to die but in order to begin something new. (*PA* 181)

Clearly, the priority of acting with others is in direct opposition to Heidegger's emphasis on the need to solitarily examine one's mortality in order to be authentic. In addition, Villa asserts that the apparent 'whitewash' of Heidegger's views in 'Heidegger at Eighty', is really an indictment of Heidegger's professional thinking and his inability to judge politically.[47] Heidegger was a great philosopher, but this is his most important political failing, because he fails to keep his mind upon politics and suffers from political thoughtlessness.[48] Villa claims that Arendt may be guilty of failing to underscore the connection between thinking and political judgment in her essay 'honouring' Heidegger, but that Arendt's ultimate position on Heidegger's work is strong criticism of Heidegger's evasion of politics and his lack of proper political judgment.[49]

As far as Arendt's personal comments are concerned, her thoughts about Heidegger often emerged in her letters. Though there is admiration of Heidegger's intellectual abilities in Arendt's letters, there are also negative comments concerning Heidegger's personality and his work. In a letter to Karl Jaspers, Arendt comments on Heidegger's poor treatment of his mentor Edmund Husserl, who was Jewish and a close friend and influence upon Heidegger. Arendt thought that Heidegger had to sign and circulate a letter to Husserl during his rectorship, informing Husserl that he was no longer welcome at the university. Arendt believes that Heidegger should have resigned the rectorship, rather than support the removal of his friend from his university. Arendt considered Heidegger to be a 'potential murder' because Arendt suspected that the fact of Husserl receiving the letter from Heidegger, rather than a stranger, would nearly have killed Husserl (*JC* 47). She also thought that Heidegger lacked character, often lied and was unable to express his political responsibility during the war years because he was liable to 'fast-talk himself out of everything unpleasant'(*JC* 142). In her personal journal, Arendt wrote a piece called 'Heidegger the Fox', which tells a moral fable about a fox that could not tell the difference between a trap and a non-trap and builds a trap that everyone had to step into in order to visit him. She claims 'nobody knows the nature of traps better than one who sits in a trap his whole life long', suggesting that Heidegger's philosophy was misguided because it failed to take politics seriously and merely was some sort of mental game, or trap (*PA* 543). She comments in 1952 that she thinks that Heidegger's strong influence on German academia in Heidelberg was 'disastrous and disgustingly idiotic', and finds persons who idolize Heidegger's thought to be problematic, even though both she and her husband, Heinrich Blücher, kept up with Heidegger's academic work throughout their lives (*WFW* 212). Perhaps her most revealing statement about her relationship with Heidegger occurs in a letter to Jaspers in 1961. Arendt admits to deceiving Heidegger about her intellectual ability and feigning that her intellectual work was entirely dependent upon Heidegger, until she could no longer pretend this was the case (*JC* 457). Apparently, he was upset with her and, though she was angry at first, she felt she deserved his scorn for deceiving him for so long.

Arendt and Jaspers never came to terms over Heidegger. She was particularly troubled by the conflict between Karl Jaspers and Martin Heidegger, who despite being close before the war, had a falling out over Heidegger's Nazism. Arendt, for the most part, sided with Jaspers, but after 1950, maintained a friendship with both of them. Arendt initially tried to reunite them, but gave up after a while. Arendt's and Jaspers' correspondence reveal that Jaspers was harder on Heidegger, and at one point, Jaspers cut off all correspondence with Heidegger. Jaspers reacted to Arendt's assertion that Heidegger should be left in peace, by claiming that it was politically dangerous to do so as many other academics were justifying their behaviour by referencing Heidegger (*JC* 161–2, 629). Overall, Arendt's letters suggest that despite of her admiration for Heidegger's intellectual abilities, in later life, she visited Jaspers more, wrote to Jaspers more, was closer to Jaspers, and that she certainly respected Jaspers' intellectual work more. In 1957, she states that her dear most honoured one, which was the salutation that she used when writing to Jaspers, was the only person who educated her when she was young (*JC* 331). Her relationship to Heidegger is certainly complicated, but Arendt frequently commented that the strongest intellectual influence upon her was Karl Jaspers because of his dedicated interest in politics.

LITTLE ROCK AND AMERICAN RACE ISSUES

There is a growing body of literature that examines the role of race within Arendt's work, particularly her treatment of Africans in *The Origins of Totalitarianism* and her discussions of African Americans in the United States. The greatest controversy on this point emerged over Arendt's discussion of the school integration that took place in Little Rock, Arkansas in 1957. In her article 'Reflections on Little Rock', Arendt expresses the view that she is against school integration, mainly, because it shifts the burden of solving race problems to children, rather than adults (*RJ* 203). Prompted by a photo of a young Negro girl having to face the combative crowds on her way home from an integrated school, Arendt thinks that it was a disturbing experience that she would not want to expose her own child to, if she was the mother of a Negro child (*RJ* 193). It is Arendt's view that the coerced school integration asks children to change and improve the world and take on burdens that adults have proven unable to do, forcing children into mature situations that could be too much for them.

In addition, Arendt controversially claims that the matter of whom parents choose to educate their children with is a social, rather than political, issue. For Arendt, discrimination in regards to education is acceptable so long as there are other schooling options, and Arendt thinks it is a mistake to start to improve race relations through school integration because it takes rights away from parents. Arendt believes that forced integration deprives parents of rights to free association (*RJ* 212). Oddly, Arendt thinks that social discrimination is acceptable because it allows 'like' to attract 'like' and permits free association between individuals (*RJ* 205). For instance, Arendt states that Jews should be allowed to vacation together and that exclusions such as these should be permitted. What she does not think is tolerable are exclusions concerning things that everyone needs to pursue their daily lives, like being able to sit anywhere on a bus or train, or having access to facilities in business districts. Arendt believes that if the Supreme Court decision *Brown* v. *Board of Education*, which mandated school integration, is to be taken seriously, it would actually challenge the right to private education at all, because every private school is a type of segregated school (*RJ* 212). Interestingly, in 1933, Arendt argues for a fully Jewish school system to make Jewish students who emigrated from Germany feel welcome and help avoid the problems of forced integration (*JW* 19). Arendt also claims that *Brown* v. *Board of Education* decision mistakenly makes education a federal problem in the United States, when education is typically under the control of the states (*RJ* 210). Curiously, Arendt asserts that the legality of interracial marriage was a more important issue to tackle for civil rights, since it concerned the choices of adults and interfered with rights of individuals to decide with whom to spend their lives. Finally, with an appeal to objectivity and disinterestedness, Arendt proclaims in her preliminary remarks to 'Reflections on Little Rock', which were written two years later, when the article was finally published, that:

> oppressed minorities were never the best judges of their order of priorities in such matters and there are many instances when they preferred to fight for social opportunity rather than for basic human or political rights. (*PA* 232)

Clearly, statements such as these are offensive to those who are fighting for equality in ways that Arendt deems to be social.

Immediately following its publication in 1959, and even before its release, 'Reflections on Little Rock' received criticism, which is why its publication was initially delayed for two years. Interestingly, there are few complaints about Arendt's concern that integration of the public schools places an unfair burden upon children: a point that was lost in the early reaction to her work.[50] Right away, political scientists David Spitz and Melvin Tumin and philosopher Sidney Hook, criticized Arendt's article with the broader complaint that questioned the viability of her position concerning the distinct and separate spheres between the public, private and social. For Hook, equality is something that involves the social and economic sphere and should be regarded as a political issue.[51] Others were offended by Arendt's audacity in claiming to decide what should be important for the Civil Rights Movement. Yet, in the midst of the controversy surrounding her article, Arendt accepted the criticism made by the novelist Ralph Ellison. Ellison argues that Arendt fails to understand the ideal of sacrifice in the African-American community and the need for children to face the daily horror of the society in which they live at an early age. Ellison thinks that episodes like the integration at Little Rock are rites of passage that prepare children for the terror of their lives as blacks and help them to master their inner tensions.[52]

Arendt admits that she was wrong to assume that this form of racism in the United States was the same as the racism she suffered in her youth and that she acknowledges that she did not understand the ideal of sacrifice and the terror of the black youth in America.[53] In her preliminary remarks to the article, Arendt also claims that she was justly criticized for failing to acknowledge the importance of the role of education in the political framework of the United States (*PA* 232). Finally, she reminds the readers that she writes as an outsider and wants to make it clear that 'as a Jew I take my sympathy for the cause of the Negroes as for all oppressed or under-privileged peoples for granted and should appreciate it if the reader did likewise' (*PA* 232).

For many scholars, Arendt's mistakes in her Little Rock essay are symptomatic of a larger problem. Anne Norton notes a pattern in Arendt's writings that reinforce certain racisms that are perpetuated by the canon of intellectual thought in which Arendt's work is based. Despite Arendt's personal avowal of sympathy with the cause of African Americans, Norton finds many features in Arendt's thought that preserve the unjust social order, particularly in her treatment of Africans in *The Origins of Totalitarianism* and in her treatment of blacks in her essays on American culture and society, including 'Reflections on Little Rock'.[54] Not just in the Little Rock essay, but throughout Arendt's work, Norton thinks that Arendt dismisses African history, literature, languages and readily ascribes 'academic inferiority to black students, and squalor, crime, and ignorance to the black community' often equating blackness with the givenness of nature, which is a negative concept in Arendt's work in contrast to political action.[55] Joy James concurs with this view and argues that Arendt's political categories that are derived from the Greek *polis* 'mask racism . . . by concealing the private realm of domestic service, field labor, and child-rearing as the designated world for racialized peoples (and women)'.[56] Robert Bernasconi agrees that Arendt's work involves racial blindness, arguing that Arendt's positive interpretation of the American Revolution does not take seriously what she calls the 'social question' of black slavery. For Bernasconi, it is difficult to understand how Arendt can claim that there is a lack of misery in the United States, as compared to France, because of the existence of slavery.[57]

Richard H. King, among others, asserts that many of Arendt's misconceptions concerning the situation in Little Rock are due to the fact that she thought of black racism in America in terms of her experience of antisemitism in Europe as an educated, middle-class, European Jew. In this regard, King believes Arendt's 'own experience, when it was mapped onto American and southern realities led her astray', and that Königsberg and Little Rock have more differences than similarities.[58] Marriage rights are important to Arendt personally, because she married a gentile, which would not have been allowed in Nazi Germany. Subsequently, Arendt argues for the importance of marriage rights, despite the fact that Negroes thought interracial marriage was not high on their list of priorities.[59] Arendt attended an integrated school where her mother insisted that if she was attacked as a Jew, she must defend herself as a Jew. However, King notes that protests of antisemitism would not put Arendt or her mother's life in danger in pre-Nazi Europe, like it would in Little Rock, Arkansas in 1957.[60] Arendt also fails to see that school integration in Arkansas is not a repetition of the parvenu status that assimilated Jews in Europe may have sought by entering integrated schools.[61] Further, King believes that Arendt does not acknowledge that schools are a part of the public realm and therefore, are legitimate sites of political action, such as in the case of Little Rock.[62]

Other scholars, like Kristie McClure think of Arendt's article on Little Rock as an example of political judgment, even in its failure. For McClure, Arendt expresses her opinions in the Little Rock essay and it is up to the spectators to insert their contrasting opinions in order to make sense of school integration. Though Arendt was read as making authoritative claims that were meant to convince others to have the same opinion, McClure sees it as the beginning of a political conversation.[63] If Arendt is guilty of ignorance of African-American history and of equating her experience of racism with the southern black experience, then it is up to the community to disagree with her and discuss the issue in hopes of correcting it. Arendt's controversial findings are then beneficial in bringing people together to discuss the problem of segregated schools, racism and productive ways to solve these problems. In general, Arendt's views on Little Rock have alienated persons from her overall theory, and this trend continues in Arendt's lack of attention to feminist concerns.

FEMINISM

In addition to criticisms concerning Arendt's discussion of American race issues, Arendt's work has also been a flash point for feminist discussions. Arendt herself was not in favour of feminism. In general, Arendt disagrees with social movements that answer a variety of political questions from the viewpoint of a specific group. As Elisabeth Young-Bruehl notes, Arendt did not view herself as a feminist and was sceptical of any political movement based upon a single issue, especially if that issue ignored the public and private distinction.[64] This was one of Arendt's criticisms of the Zionist movement, in that it failed to see a larger political picture beyond the interests of the group. However, Arendt did acknowledge that it was problematic if women did not receive equal pay for equal work, but aside from the pay issue and the unfair burden of housework upon women, Arendt regarded women as having already been emancipated as early as 1933 (*EU* 66). According to her friend Hans Jonas, Arendt actually thought that men were the weaker sex, since they are more likely to be seduced by intellectual theory that was disconnected from the world.[65]

In general, Arendt's discussion of feminist issues is particularly negative. In an interview in 1964, she states that she is old fashioned when it comes to women's liberation and that she thinks

> there are certain occupations that are improper for women, that do not become them, if I may put it that way. It just doesn't look good when a woman gives orders. She should try not to get into such a situation if she wants to remain feminine. (*PA* 4)

Arendt did, however, claim that she was not sure if she was right about this point and that this attitude did not limit her own life in any way (*PA* 4). When she was put in the position of being the first woman to achieve something, she was very uncomfortable. Arendt was annoyed when it was publicized that she would be the first woman with the rank of full professor at Princeton when she lectured there in 1959, and she tried to kill the newspaper story covering that fact (*JC* 357). According to Elisabeth Young-Bruehl, Arendt resented being cast in the role of 'exception woman', just as she criticized the problem of being an 'exception' Jew.[66] Because of attitudes like these, some scholars have thought that Arendt's work is hostile to feminist aims. In regard to her theoretical claims, feminists have taken issue with Arendt's separation of the public and the private, since it seems to classify gender injustices at home as 'private' and therefore excludes them from being a political issue. John McGowan also points out that Arendt uses the term 'man' and 'mankind' to refer to the whole of humanity throughout the entirety of her work, further distancing her theory from feminist concerns.[67]

In *Feminist Interpretations of Hannah Arendt*, Mary G. Dietz argues that the feminist discussion of Hannah Arendt's work tends to classify her work according to the binary categories of sex, and Dietz calls these interpretations either phallocratic or gynocentric.[68] Those thinkers focusing on the phallocratic Arendt, like Adrienne Rich, Mary O'Brien, Hannah Pitkin and Wendy Brown criticize Arendt's theory for favouring males in society and reinforcing traditional gender roles. Since Arendt's discussion of politics is grounded in ancient Athens, many argue that the only way in which freedom emerges politically is if there is a domestic or slave labor force ready to manage the daily tasks so that some free citizens can participate politically. Arguing that women get sided with the private sphere and the needs of the body, these thinkers criticize Arendt for prioritizing the public sphere of males over the traditional roles of women in society. Adrienne Rich asserts that Arendt completely ignores the fact that private household labor is traditionally associated with females, while the realm of political action is traditionally associated with males. Rich claims that Arendt's notion of the 'political actor', is the product of a 'diet of masculine ideology', and faults Arendt for falling into the masculine trap.[69]

Inspired by difference feminism that supports the idea that men and women differ significantly, but should be valued equally, Dietz believes that other feminists take the opposite position, like Terry Winant, Nancy Hartsock, Jean Bethke Elshtain and Sara Ruddick, who stress the concepts of natality, love, plurality, worldliness and find positive aspects to Arendt's thought for feminist concerns based on the feminine nature of her concepts. Often, these thinkers look to Arendt's *Rahel Varnhagen* as a book that captures the struggles of a Jewish woman in a concrete manner that takes into account the body, gender and ethnicity, instead of describing the human subject in an abstract and universal way. Despite the fact that its title masks the fact that it includes essays about women, others thinkers look to *Men in Dark Times* as a valuable resource that discusses the impact of individual women, like Rosa Luxemburg, on politics.

Finally, Dietz characterizes a third type of reading of Arendt, the post-modern or 'diversity' readings, that complicate gender and try to displace and question traditional gender categories. Dietz argues that by trying to mobilize Arendtian politics for feminist concerns inspired by identity politics in the phallocratic and gynocentric readings, feminists miss the emancipatory potential in Arendt's theory that rejects the 'what-ness', or essence, of gender identity in favour of 'who' an individual is.[70] For Dietz, Arendt's concept of political action helps to release feminist thought from dividing all human capacities into masculine and feminine categories and provides a description of politics based on spontaneity and unpredictability that can be liberating.[71]

Lastly, scholars like Ann M. Lane and Bat-Ami Bar On believe that Arendt's work is grounded in Jewish experience, which can be relevant for feminist concerns.[72] Bat-Ami Bar On states that even though Arendt was not a feminist, 'there is a lot she has to offer to feminist theorizing', since being a Jew was central to her thinking. Bar On argues that that the impact of the Nazis on Arendt's life may have decentred gender concerns for her, which is somewhat understandable.[73] However, Elisabeth Young-Bruehl disagrees with this positive view. Though Young-Bruehl agrees that Arendt's view of feminism was influenced by the centrality of Jewish concerns in her life, she does not think that this is beneficial to feminist thinking. Young-Bruehl believes that Arendt thinks more as a Jew than as a woman, which leads to the consequence of Arendt construing all types of oppression as forms of antisemitism, masking the differences between certain types of oppression.[74] Whereas the collapse of the public and private is central to an anti-totalitarian movement that would prevent antisemitism, it is not an appropriate model for many feminist issues which need to address the intersection of the public and the private, and Arendt fails to see how her theory does not work out for feminist concerns. Therefore, Young-Bruehl believes that Arendt's work is crucial for antisemitism, but not as useful for feminism.[75] Though the value of her theory for feminism has sparked controversy, the most contentious claims against Arendt, however, are made against her discussion of Jewish concerns.

JEWISH THOUGHT

The greatest controversy over Hannah Arendt's work concerns her discussion and treatment of Jewish issues. Often throughout her career, Arendt was disparaged by various Jewish groups and thinkers for the way that she handled and discussed Jewish subject matters. Due to her criticisms of Zionism and the infamous Eichmann controversy, Arendt was considered to be 'person non grata' in Israeli intellectual circles for many years, though she did travel to Israel regularly to visit family (*JW* 519).[76] Despite its potential to appeal to a Jewish audience, her book on Eichmann was not translated into Hebrew until 2000. According to Ron H. Feldman, Arendt was neither fully inside nor outside her Jewish or European heritage, but she used her outsider status as a unique vantage point to evaluate and criticize both Jewish issues and the European intellectual heritage.[77] Even so, Arendt did not think of herself as existentially outside of her Jewish background. Arendt accepted and defended the fact that she was Jewish and unlike the parvenu, she did not try to escape this fact through being an exception. When she married Heinrich Blücher, she kept her professional name of 'Arendt' to indicate that she was a Jew (*JC* 29). She thought that being a Jew was an indisputable fact of her life and she never wished to change or deny it, insisting that if one is attacked as a Jew, one must defend oneself as a Jew (*PA* 392). An appeal to universal human rights does not work as a defence, because it relinquishes the very thing for which one is being attacked. Further complicating the issue, Arendt did not believe in Judaism, or the religion of the Jewish people, and made a distinction between the ethnicity of being Jewish and the beliefs of Judaism.[78] Feldman describes Arendt's attitude by stating that for her, Jewishness was an existential given that could not be denied, while Judaism was a set of beliefs that could be chosen.[79] Arendt did believe in God, but she also stated that traditional organized religion 'holds nothing whatsoever for me anymore' (*JC* 166). Despite her rejection of Judaism, Arendt considered the Jewish question to be central to her work and Jennifer Ring argues that unbeknownst to her, Arendt's scholarly concerns and questions are rooted in classical Jewish themes.[80]

Rahel Varnhagen, *The Origins of Totalitarianism*, *Eichmann in Jerusalem* and many of Arendt's essays comment directly upon Jewish concerns, while her other political philosophy handles the same issues in a more abstract way by proposing political structures that would avoid the catastrophe of totalitarianism and its promotion of antisemitism or other forms of intolerant and hostile attitudes. In her early essays on the Jewish question, Arendt sought to explain the rise of antisemitism in Europe and to encourage Jews to become more politically active. Arendt discussed the work of Bernard Lazare and his view that the Jew must become a conscious pariah who acts politically and becomes a rebel. In contrast, she condemned the quest to become an 'exception' Jew and discussed how this strategy failed to respond adequately to antisemitism. She criticized the famous writer, Stephan Zweig, for trying unsuccessfully to hide in his fame and maintained that since the war, the pariah and parvenu were in the same boat, without legal rights (*JW* 296). The statelessness caused by the war often led Jews to seek assimilation into the new nation, but for Arendt, the Jews needed to stop falling into the trap of evading one's status as a Jew. Often, she urged Jewish involvement in politics and was adamant that a Jewish army, under a Jewish flag, consisting of members from several nations, was necessary to combat the Nazis as Jews, rather than as French or English citizens. Arendt thought that the Jewish Army would prove that the Jews were engaged in politics and that they were no different than anyone else (*JW* 138). Being members of a Jewish army would also unite them under a flag and not force them to assimilate to a different national status. She praised the uprising in the Warsaw ghetto in which Jews fought back against the Nazis and maintained the battle for several weeks. She thought that the Warsaw ghetto battle was an instance of honour and glory, which foreshadowed the same language that she later used to describe political action (*JW* 199). She supported the creation of a commonwealth of European nations after the war because she thought that Jews could have representation in a commonwealth as a legitimate political body (*JW* 130). Arendt became sympathetic to the Zionist movement during the Second World War because she believed that they were the only ones who were ready to fight back against Nazism as Jews, rather than trying to be assimilated. It was unlike Arendt to join a group, but she claimed that she was a Zionist from 1933–1943, but then broke with them for philosophical reasons.[81]

The person who introduced her to Zionism was Kurt Blumenfeld, who like Arendt herself, was a Jew that was connected to the intellectual community. To assist the Zionists, Arendt offered her apartment in Berlin to aid persons who were fleeing Hitler's regime.[82]

However, Arendt's main assignment for the Zionists was to collect information at the Prussian State Library concerning overt antisemitism in private clubs, nongovernmental organizations and professional societies.[83] The report on the propaganda and antisemitism of these groups was to be used at the next Zionist conference to show the extremely precarious status of Jews in Germany. She was chosen by Blumenfeld for the task because since she was not known to be a formal member of Zionists, the group would not be found out if she was caught.[84] Arendt happily took on the task and was glad to finally do something active in relation to the oppression of the Nazis. She was caught several months later, but befriended her interviewer, was released and was able to escape. After immigrating to France, Arendt gave up intellectual work, to do what she called 'social work' for Zionist groups, including moving Jewish children to Palestine during the war. All and all, Arendt worked for Zionist and Jewish organizations for 20 years.[85] After the war, though, Arendt broke with the Zionists over a number of issues. According to Richard J. Bernstein, Arendt was motivated to break with the Zionists when they failed to include equality in their politics by being pro-Israel at the expense of Arabs.[86] Her break from Zionism, however, was never in full, and Bernstein claims that Arendt thought of herself as being part of the loyal opposition to the Zionists, rather than anti-Zionist.[87]

Arendt has a variety of disagreements with Zionist groups. As has been already mentioned, Arendt is suspicious of groups that address politics from the perspective of their private concerns. Though Arendt strongly supports Jewish solidarity, it could not be at the expense of common sense and judgment from the perspective of what is best for the community at large. In terms of Zionist philosophy, Arendt rejects the view of the famous founder of modern Zionism, Theodor Herzl, who believed that the cause of antisemitism was due to the laws of history and the existence of an 'eternal antisemitism' towards the Jews. Arendt criticizes this idea in various essays as well as in *The Origins of Totalitarianism*. If it is true that something like 'eternal antisemitism' exists, then it would be impossible for it to be corrected through political action and it places the source of this problem outside of human hands into the laws of history. The idea that antisemitism is 'natural' is a repugnant ideology to Arendt, especially since it implies that it cannot be cured (*JW* 353). In addition, Arendt thinks the belief in 'eternal antisemitism' was the key factor that prompted Herzl to argue for the need of a sovereign state, like

Israel, in order to escape from universal prejudice, but what Arendt contends is that Herzl did not realize that 'the country he dreamed of did not exist', as there was nowhere on earth that was isolated enough and free of a population that could be occupied by the Jewish people (*JW* 382). Finally, Arendt objects to the belief in 'eternal antisemitism' because it exempts Jews from their responsibility in historically failing to address political questions and choosing, rather, to assimilate or to seek special privileges, like the parvenu. Arendt believes that antisemitism is not the result of forces beyond human control but that it could be combated through human choice and by holding people responsible for their antisemitic attitudes. For Arendt, antisemitism 'is not a natural phenomenon but a political one' (*JW* 182).

Second, and more importantly, Arendt disagrees with the Zionists over the founding of the state of Israel that did not accommodate the Arabs in a binational Palestine (*JW* 194). She believes that to establish the state through force and to fail to give Palestinians equal rights was 'out of touch with the realities of the situation in the Near East and the world at large', because it ignored the fact that there was an Arab majority in Palestine and that the neighbouring countries also contained Arab majorities (*JW* lviii). Therefore, the Arabs would either have to accept their minority status, or emigrate. Arendt thinks that the state must promote the equal rights of all citizens, Arabs and Jews alike, which prior to the formation of Israel, could have been accomplished in a variety of ways. One idea Arendt supports is making Israel part of a federation of Mediterranean states, modelled on something like the United States, but with international state members, in which the smaller states would not be oppressed by the larger states because of the division of power (*JW* 197). This alliance would potentially include some European nations as well. Within the federation, each state would have a voice and it would diffuse the situation as being one in which Jews and Arabs needed to confront one another as exclusive enemies. Alternatively, Arendt does not endorse a strictly Arab federation, because this would make Israel a minority state. She also does not support any form of colonialist rule in Palestine by either the United States or Great Britain because it would impinge upon the freedom of both Arabs and Jews.

Arendt asserts that both the extremist Jews and extremist Arabs were at fault for the condition of the Middle East, and even though the Arabs were subject to blame in many ways, she recognized that they have legitimate complaints against the Israelis. Arendt blamed the British Mandate that separated Arabs and Jews into different areas for allowing Arabs and Jews to disregard one another because they primarily had to deal with the British. Arendt complains that the two groups did not develop a political regard or responsibility for one another and failed to understand the needs of their neighbour. Arendt thinks that this is unfortunate because at the time of the founding of Israel, there was the potential for both groups to work together and constitute the state with equal representation of all interests. Cooperation between Jews and Arabs in the Middle East could have been the basis for a true sovereignty and independence, but both sides have failed to see their neighbour as a concrete human being. Arendt considers both the Jews and the Arabs to be stubborn and unwilling to compromise, and she thinks that each side must give up their nationalistic claims or all sovereignty would be lost in the region (*JW* 430). In 1948, Arendt advocates that terrorist groups on both sides should be eliminated and their terrorist acts punished as quickly as possible, to help heal the divide between the groups (*JW* 401). Clearly, many Zionists are against Arendt's views, but the main problem for Arendt was that the Zionists, who promoted Israeli concerns, but denied Arabs political rights, were repeating the kind of racist, or what she called, 'chauvinistic' politics that gave rise to Nazism in the first place (*JW* 393). Arendt fears that the failure to recognize Arab's claims did not cure antisemitism as someone like Herzl desired, but merely transformed it into anti-Zionism. According to Cristina Sánchez Muñoz, the main issue for Arendt concerns the fact that she was against the idea of the political community being founded upon natural, rather than political bonds.[88] Founding the state on natural bonds, like being Jewish, is exclusionary and does not recognize the equality of all people or their freedom to act.

Even though Arendt rejects the formation of a Jewish state that did not grant equal rights to Palestinians, she did believe in the legitimacy and need for the foundation of a Jewish homeland, as opposed to a Jewish state. For Arendt, the homeland was more important because it would be a cultural centre that would recognize Jewish accomplishments. Arendt fears that by transferring the needs of the Jews into an issue of land or place, the emphasis on culture would be lost and the Jews would need to concentrate much more on security against the hostile Arabs, instead of issues of cultural importance (*JW* 396). As early as 1947, Arendt suspected that things in Palestine would not work out (*JC* 91). In the end, Arendt thinks that certain elements in Zionism were dangerous and 'should be discarded for the sake of Israel', because there was an urgent need to keep the struggle for freedom free from fascism (*JW* 171, 479).

Finally, the greatest controversy over Arendt's ideas concerned Arendt's analysis of the Eichmann trial. As Phillip Hansen comments, *Eichmann in Jerusalem* may turn out to be Arendt's most memorable book, not for its theoretical ideas, but because of the heated controversy that it elicited after it was first published as a series in the magazine *The New Yorker*.[89] The public criticism of Arendt on this issue was harsh and sustaining. Intellectually, there were two main issues of concern. The first concern was the worry that Arendt denied the diabolical nature of Eichmann's acts. This also meant that she changed her views concerning radical evil as articulated in *The Origins of Totalitarianism*, but this change of position was not the main reason for the controversy. Many thought that the phrase 'banality of evil', was offensive because it trivialized the Holocaust and Eichmann's role in it. By describing evil as banal, many accused Arendt of excusing Eichmann's behaviour, which amounted to an accusation against the victims and a pardon for the executioner.[90] Some even thought that Arendt was suggesting that there was an Eichmann within each of us that would appear under the right conditions, though Arendt denied this claim.

It is clear, however, that throughout *Eichmann in Jerusalem*, Arendt held Eichmann accountable for his behaviour and the phrase 'banality of evil', was not meant to suggest that the evil that was perpetrated was banal, or that the suffering of evil was banal, but that the banality of evil emerged from a lack of thought on Eichmann's part (*JW* 478–9). In an interview in 1964, Arendt states 'nothing could be further from my mind than to trivialize the greatest catastrophe of our century' (*JW* 487). All and all, Dagmar Barnouw believes that it was the strange combination of clarity and obscurity in Arendt's writing that allowed readers to react with hostility and to misunderstand Arendt's intentions.[91] Barnouw thinks that Arendt sought to communicate and understand the mentality of someone like Eichmann, while still holding him responsible, which contrasts with her accusers, who chose withdrawal and silence as the only possible response to Eichmann's behaviour. Barnouw thinks that Arendt's accusers were unable to understand what Eichmann did, favouring a simpler view that demonized his actions.[92] Arendt chalked up the misunderstanding of her intentions to the fact that it was easier for some people to attribute evil to a metaphysical principle like demonic evil, than to an average man (*JW* 488).

The second and most controversial issue over her book on the Eichmann trial concerned the apparent denouncement of the *Judenräte*, or Jewish Councils, and the role some of them played in the Holocaust by cooperating with the Nazis. Many felt that Arendt blamed the Jews for the Holocaust in this section of her book. Her critics also contended that she was overly sympathetic with Eichmann and overly critical of the Jewish councils. According to Richard J. Bernstein, the most controversial claims that Arendt made were her statement that the Jewish leaders had a role in the destruction of their people, but also, that if the Jews had stronger leaders, the numbers of the dead would have been smaller.[93] Several people thought that Arendt condemned the Jewish councils in a harsher manner than her condemnation of Eichmann. Stephen J. Whitfield asserts that Arendt's view was slanted and that readers were not given an idea of how difficult it was to go underground, and that she could have focused on the good work that some of the Jewish councils accomplished.[94] Overall, Whitfield believes that her emphasis should have been on the 'intensity of the Nazi desire to kill', regardless of the response of the Jewish leaders.[95] One of her harshest critics, Gershom Scholem, reacted to Arendt's tone in the book, which he claims made him unable to take her thesis more seriously.[96] In a letter to Arendt, Scholem accuses Arendt of having no love for the Jewish people and of hating Zionism.[97] In her defence, Arendt notes that she called the questions that arose during the trial concerning the collusion of the Jews cruel, and she claims that the reason that she reported the complicity of the Jewish Councils was because it was discussed in the trial, but also, because it gave some insight into the total moral collapse that occurred in Europe during the war (*EJ* 111).

The controversy over the Eichmann book, prompted the writing of a reactionary book, which Arendt claims was funded by Zionist organizations in an effort to condemn her work. The book by Jacob Robinson called *And the Crooked Shall be Made Straight* claimed to have found over 400 factual errors in Arendt's book and aimed to question the intellectual integrity of Arendt's book in order to dismiss it entirely. Interestingly, in Walter Z. Laqueur's review of *And the Crooked Shall be Made Straight*, Laqueur argues that the case against Arendt was not entirely made. While factual errors are certainly problematic, part of the problem was that she did not have access to the resources that Robinson did and she did not have a team of researchers to investigate many of the facts in her report, like Robinson. Laqueur asserts that despite the factual errors, the main philosophical ideas, such as the existence of the 'banality of evil', were not successfully attacked by Robinson.[98] Laqueur notes a sense of imbalance in Robinson's book that mainly attacked Arendt's work over details, but did not persuade the reader concerning the broader issues of the book. Lacquer concludes that Robinson attacked Arendt 'not so much for what she said, but for how she said it'.[99] Arendt's reaction to Robinson's book was that she thought it was completely biased because Robinson was a consultant for the prosecution in Eichmann's trial and he could not objectively report on the facts of the trail. She was astounded that he was able to get his book published (*JW* 499, 507). She saw Robinson's work as a type of image-making that sought to cast Arendt and her book as evil, and she noted that if Robinson's goal was to stop discussion about her book, then he failed (*JW* 509–10).

Arendt's overall response to the Eichmann controversy was shock and confusion. Though there were many who supported her book and found it interesting, there was also a great amount of contentious criticism. In fact, a French publication, *Observateaur*, printed a headline asking whether Arendt was a Nazi, though it seems they did it mainly to sell more copies and were not asking the question earnestly (*BF* 198). Often, Arendt asserted that those who attacked her had not read her book, especially the section concerning the Jewish councils. Arendt claimed that she was 'attacked . . . for what I never said', and she admitted that there was a serious breakdown in communication between the author and reader in her book on Eichmann (*RJ* 17). Arendt saw her role at the trail as an observer who was there to report the facts. In her defence, Arendt emphasized that the reason for discussing the issue of the Jewish councils was because it was raised in the trail by Mr Gideon Haussner from the Israeli public prosecutor's office and that she did not view the book as an opportunity to investigate the role of the Jews in the Holocaust, but that it merely served as a report on the trial. Arendt underscored her statement in her book that she thought the repeated questions about the non-resistance of the Jews were 'cruel and silly' (*EJ* 9). She also maintained that she did not discuss the positive roles of the Jewish councils during the war because they were not discussed in the trial.[100] Answering a written interview question, Arendt claimed that she believed that the Jews, including the Jewish councils, were objectively, not subjectively, helpless in fighting against the Holocaust, though she also believed that the members of the councils should have admitted their helplessness and resigned from their duties (*JW* 494). In response to Gershom Scholem's attacks, she asserted that much of what he argued was false and not contained in her book. She did, however, admit that did not have a love of the Jewish people because she did not love any collective, but only persons who were her friends.[101] Still, she continued that the wrong that was done to the Jews grieved her more than it would with other people because she was one of them.[102] According to Elisabeth Young-Bruehl, the controversy in the *New Yorker* continued for three years, causing Arendt to lose long-time friends, including Kurt Blumenfeld.[103] Arendt's defence that she was merely reporting the facts did not satisfy her critics, since the line between fact and interpretation in the book was vague, and clearly there was a lot of editorializing amidst the reporting of the facts.[104] But, despite this breakdown in communications, Arendt claimed that she would not write the book differently because she thought she was reporting the facts, so she believed that she was being attacked for being the messenger. Arendt answered that her only alternative would be to remain silent altogether and she did not believe that writing her report differently would have accomplished a major change in reception of the book (*JW* 478).

In nearly all of the cases that Arendt's writing is seen as most controversial, a similar critique often emerges. Those objecting to Arendt's positions often mention an insensitive tone in her writing, particularly in her most controversial works. In Raymond Aron's review of *The Origins of Totalitarianism,* he claims that Arendt 'affects a tone of haughty superiority regarding things and men'.[105] This issue worsened in the Eichmann book. Stephen J. Whitfield claims that Jewish readers found the book unfeeling, cold and abstract.[106] Gershom Scholem describes a flippancy of tone in the Eichmann book that is 'unimaginably inappropriate', given the subject matter of the book.[107] Walter Laqueur argues that the judgments against her work would be less harsh if it 'were not for the conceit and the contempt, which appear all along'.[108] In general, the message of certain of her works seems to have been missed by some of her readers, particularly when her works are analysed in isolation from one another.

Although Arendt recognized that there was a great deal of confusion between herself and some of her readers, Arendt did not think that this problem was easily corrected. She admitted that she did think that Eichmann was a 'buffoon' and that certain of his responses made her laugh out loud in court (*PA* 15). She claimed that persons who thought that these issues could only be discussed in a solemn tone of voice would not understand her work at all. Arendt believed that she could do nothing about the perceived problem with her tone because she was being intentionally ironic and that those who are upset about this fact had an objection to her personality and style (*PA* 16). The ironic tone was not a misunderstanding, and her audience understood her perfectly. They just did not agree with her choice of tone (*PA* 16).

Arendt certainly presumed much of her readers. Arendt did not stress the fact that she was interested in equality and in stopping racist politics nearly enough and often took for granted that the reader was familiar with the rest of her work. She claimed that the writing process came easy for her and that she did not write until she had an issue completely sorted out in her mind. She compared this type of writing to taking dictation from herself (*PA* 5). She stated: 'usually I write it all down only once. And that goes relatively quickly, since it really depends only on how fast I can type' (*PA* 5). She mentioned to her friend Mary McCarthy that she hated writing a second draft of a book and tried to avoid it (*BF* 131). Jaspers also criticized Arendt's dissertation for its lack of attention to scholarly details, and according to Lotte Kohler and Hans Saner, Arendt had a tendency of letting the horses run away with her when she had an idea (*JC* xx). In spite of all her controversial positions, it seems that what Arendt is guilty of most of all, is failing to have the patience necessary to truly communicate her thoughts to her reader, so that she would not be as frequently misunderstood. Arendt was so passionate about thinking that she got lost in it, and she failed to have the patience to trudge through the details and rewrite her drafts in order to avoid some of the more heated aspects to some of these disputes. Her ideas would no doubt still spark controversy, and many of her claims may be mistaken, but some of the more contentious issues could potentially have been avoided with more attention to the details and familiarizing the reader with her positions in other works.

Regardless of all the controversies concerning her thought, Hannah Arendt's influence cannot be denied. The amount of scholarship on Arendt is astounding, grows every year, and it is apparent that many of her readers did not think that her tone was problematic, but generally assumed that her interests were to increase freedom and equality between persons and combat totalitarian policies. Clearly, Arendt's thought inspires people to think about issues, and in some respects, seems surprisingly on the mark concerning various political problems that have arisen, even after her death. Her adamant attitude towards the importance of politics and rejection of totalitarianism and forms of fascist thinking continue to remind us how important it is to preserve a space for free action in which plurality is acknowledged and celebrated. Even though her theory may have certain difficulties, it serves as a reminder that political issues are contentious and Arendt herself supports free and open debate about politics, even if it is in disagreement with her own views. In that way, the disputes concerning her work are beneficial, especially if they contribute to further understanding of the issues and prompt persons to think, to be more informed spectators, and to politically act in better ways. Arendt's scholarly interests were not meant to explain politics in abstraction, but she was deeply passionate about the possibility of a better world. Her love for the world and for thinking motivated her to speak out against totalitarianism and to try to articulate better ways for understanding politics. Since every person is a miracle for Arendt, each individual has the possibility for improving upon the world. Hannah Arendt left her unique mark by contributing significantly to the political discussion.

NOTES

INTRODUCTION

1. Once Arendt discovered that Jaspers had survived the war, she sent many care packages to both him and his wife in order to get them through the immediate postwar years. This expression of kindness brought them close together and initiated a lifelong friendship between Hannah Arendt and Karl and Gertrud Jaspers. Jaspers claimed that the only conversations that had a profound effect on his life besides those with wife, were with Arendt (*JC* 262). He told Arendt in a letter 'you have understood me, together with Gertrud—no one has done that before. And it is entirely and absolutely true' (*JC* 356).
2. Elisabeth Young-Bruehl, *Hannah Arendt: For the Love of the World* (New Haven: Yale University Press, 1982) 435.
3. Young-Bruehl 106.
4. Young-Bruehl 155.
5. Arendt's native language was German, but in addition to English, she also was fluent in French, and understood ancient Greek, Latin, Hebrew, Yiddish and Italian to a degree.
6. Karl Jaspers considered Arendt's farewell to philosophy to be a joke, even though she seemed serious about it. He also disagreed that philosophers were not serious about politics (*JC* 572).
7. Young-Bruehl 403.
8. Arendt is also influenced by her husband, Heinrich Blücher. She attended many of his lectures, but since he did not write philosophy and preferred to teach, it is difficult to tell how much influence he had upon her thinking.
9. Hannah Arendt was responsible for Benjamin's work surviving the war because she smuggled it to the United States and was integral in getting it published.
10. Margaret Canovan, *The Political Thought of Hannah Arendt* (New York: Harcourt Brace Jovanovich, 1974) 53.
11. Hannah Arendt, 'On Hannah Arendt', *Hannah Arendt: The Recovery of the Public World*, ed. Melvyn A. Hill (New York: St Martin's Press, 1979) 303.
12. Arendt in Hill 303.
13. Arendt in Hill 338.

CHAPTER ONE
TOTALITARIANISM AND THE BANALITY OF EVIL

1. Young-Bruehl 211.
2. Margaret Canovan, 'Arendt's Theory of Totalitarianism: A Reassessment', *The Cambridge Companion to Arendt*, ed. Dana Villa (Cambridge: Cambridge University Press, 2000) 26.
3. Arendt's *The Origins of Totalitarianism* and other essays do not use the spelling of 'anti-Semitism', but rather, 'antisemitism'. According to Jerome Kohn, who references Arendt's footnote from an essay called 'Antisemitism', Arendt believed that Semite was a linguistic term that later became an anthropological and ethnic one. Since there does not exist a movement or ideology called 'Semitism', she thinks that anti-Semitism, as its opposite, is a misnomer (*JW* xxxiii). In this book, I have followed those spellings that Arendt used for technical concepts like antisemitism. She also used the American spelling of labor and judgment in her work.
4. Canovan in Villa 30.
5. Though Arendt had completed most of the work on this book during the war, it was not published until 1957.
6. Mihály Vajda, 'Between Pariah and Parvenu: Hannah Arendt on Assimilation of the Jews', *Graduate Faculty Philosophy Journal* 21 (1999): 117.
7. It should be noted that Arendt's position has been criticized because it appears to downplay the horrors of colonialism in their own right, by merely discussing colonialism as a preparatory stage for totalitarianism.
8. Stephen J. Whitfield, *Into the Dark: Hannah Arendt and Totalitarianism* (Philadelphia: Temple University Press, 1980) 69.
9. Immanuel Kant, *Religion within the Limits of Reason Alone*, trans. Theodore M. Greene and Hoyt H. Hudson (New York: Harper and Row, 1960) 32.
10. Robert Mayer has an interesting article titled 'Hannah Arendt, National Socialism and the Project of Foundation' that disagrees with Arendt's interpretation of Nazism as process. He claims that Nazism did not adopt any Darwinian claims by killing what was seen as unfit to live, but that it was ultimately concerned with the preservation of the race and its blood, which is a law to prevent the motion of processes [Robert Mayer, 'Hannah Arendt, National Socialism and the Project of Foundation', *Review of Politics* 53.3 (Summer 1991): 476–9].
11. For Arendt, Homer is an early prototype of a historian who bases his work upon narratives. Homer tells the tale of the Trojans and the Achaeans, and provides us with an example of courage in the behaviour of Achilles. Without Homer, the Trojan War would be lost to history and to humanity. Through Homer's story, these individuals are remembered and 'who' they are is disclosed. But more importantly for Arendt, Homer exemplifies a storyteller whose method is unique in its impartiality (*PA* 573). Homer does not take sides, but looks on friend and foe alike equally (*PA* 573). Arendt claims that Homeric impartiality rests upon

the assumption that great events have a self-evidence to them which the poet or historian preserves. Therefore, there is no need to distort the events to favour one side of an event, or another. The oddity of Arendt's conception of history is that it is the narrative form which accomplishes the impartial rendering of the historical meaning of a particular event. Ordinarily, the narrative form would be considered to be a 'subjective' interpretation of an event. For Arendt, an impartial narrative captures an event's importance, without being biased, partial, or merely subjective.

12. Lisa Jane Disch, *Hannah Arendt and the Limits of Philosophy* (Ithaca: Cornell University Press, 1994) 109.
13. Larry May, 'Socialization and Institutional Evil', *Hannah Arendt: Twenty Years Later*, ed. Larry May and Jerome Kohn (Cambridge, MA: MIT Press, 1996) 86.
14. Norma Claire Moruzzi, *Speaking through the Mask: Hannah Arendt and the Politics of Social Identity* (Ithaca: Cornell University Press, 2000) 133.
15. Dana Villa, 'The Banality of Philosophy: Arendt and Heidegger and Eichmann', in May and Kohn 184.
16. Young-Bruehl 369.
17. Richard J. Bernstein, *Hannah Arendt and the Jewish Question* (Cambridge, MA: MIT Press, 1996) 152.
18. Initially, Arendt did not believe in the monstrosities of the concentration camps, despite the fact that she was in a French internment camp herself, before escaping to the United States (*PA* 13).
19. Arendt was bothered by the fact that after the war, it seemed that those Germans who were innocent felt guilty, and those who were criminals did not show remorse (*RJ* 28). She believed that the notion of 'collective guilt' aligned innocent persons with the criminals and exempted the guilty of their responsibility.

CHAPTER TWO
PHILOSOPHICAL THOUGHT AND THE HUMAN CONDITION

1. As Margaret Canovan notes, Arendt did not consider *The Human Condition* to be the definitive statement of her positive political theory but rather, as 'a kind of preliminary to political theory proper, an investigation of the human activities that have most bearing upon politics and have been most misunderstood' [Margaret Canovan, *Hannah Arendt: A Reinterpretation of her Political Thought* (Cambridge: Cambridge University Press, 1992) 101].
2. Dana Villa, *Politics, Philosophy, and Terror: Essays on the Thought of Hannah Arendt* (Princeton: Princeton University Press, 1999) 205.
3. Margaret Betz Hull, *The Hidden Philosophy of Hannah Arendt* (London: Routledge Curzon, 2002) 75.
4. Young-Bruehl 222.
5. Arendt believes that Kant and Jaspers are exceptions to her critique of political philosophers because both of them were keenly interested in the active life and politics. (*LOM* 83).

6. Jacques Taminiaux, *The Thracian Maid and the Professional Thinker: Arendt and Heidegger*, trans. and ed. Michael Gendre (Albany: State University of New York Press, 1997) 1.
7. Jacques Taminiaux believes that Arendt's rejection of Platonic philosophy relates to her rejection of Heidegger's philosophy since Heidegger stated in 1924 that the philosopher may indeed be the true politician (9–10).
8. As J. Peter Euben notes, Arendt's reading of Plato is somewhat 'flat-footed' in that she seems more interested in making sweeping claims about Plato, rather than noting the subtle ironies and nuances of the *Republic* ('Arendt's Hellenism', in Villa 151). While the accuracy of her interpretation of Plato and the Greeks in general are certainly in question by a number of scholars, her analysis of Plato's philosophy serves a larger purpose, which is to describe the type of politics and political theorizing that she is against.
9. Hannah Arendt, 'Philosophy and Politics', *Social Research* 57.1 (Spring 1990): 73.
10. Arendt, 'Philosophy and Politics', 80.
11. Arendt, 'Philosophy and Politics', 80.
12. Philosophers or thinkers, of course, can still be political activists, but they must momentarily leave the abstraction of philosophy behind, in order to actively engage with others and their opinions.
13. Arendt, 'Philosophy and Politics', 81.
14. Arendt in Hill 310.
15. Wayne Allen, 'Hannah Arendt and the Political Imagination', *International Philosophical Quarterly* 42.3 (2002): 367.
16. Young-Bruehl 318.
17. Young-Bruehl 318.
18. It should be noted that *The Human Condition* was the result of Arendt's attempt to write a book on the relationship between totalitarianism and Marxist thought. Concentrating on Marx led Arendt to see a conflation between labor and work in his thought, leading to a further misunderstanding of political action. Marx's theory problematically asserts that all persons are primarily laborers and that all types of politics are related to laboring. These criticisms developed into Arendt's description of politics in *The Human Condition*.
19. Earth corresponds to the activity of labor, worldliness to the activity of work, and plurality to political action, and all three correspond to natality and mortality (*HC* 7–11).
20. Though Arendt stresses that humans are conditioned beings, she underscores the fact that she is not talking about human nature, because the conditions of humanity can change, unlike human nature. Her example of the alteration of the human condition is that humans could emigrate to another planet, which would radically change the conditions of life and its corresponding activities, so Arendt's discussion is once again not focused on the essence of her topic, but on describing how the concepts of human activity have emerged and changed through time (*HC* 10).

21. According to Jerome Kohn, Arendt gets the idea for the equality and distinction of plurality that inspires political action from Montesquieu (*PP* xxvi).
22. Adriana Cavarero, *For More than One Voice: Toward a Philosophy of Vocal Expression* (Stanford: Stanford University Press, 2005) 189.
23. Arendt classifies art as fabrication and as part of work, rather than action.
24. For Jacques Taminiaux, Arendt's category of work is meant to redeem humans from the survival mode of labor, while the activity of action is meant to redeem humans from the utilitarian demands of means/end categories in work ('Athens and Rome', in Villa 169–70).
25. Arendt in Hill 305.
26. Margaret Canovan, 'Politics as Culture: Hannah Arendt and the Public Realm', *Hannah Arendt: Critical Essays*, ed. Lewis P. Hinchman and Sandra K. Hinchman (Albany: State University of New York Press, 1994) 180, and Villa, *Politics, Philosophy, Terror*, 128.
27. Cavarero 190–2.
28. See Chapter 5 for further discussion of the problem of elitism.
29. Maurizio Passerin d'Entrèves, *The Political Philosophy of Hannah Arendt* (London: Routledge, 1994) 84–5, 99.
30. It is important to note that the type of causality at work here is very weak. Arendt does not believe in teleological theories of history or predetermination in the human realm. These historical occurrences are contingent and merely logical predecessors to modern alienation, rather than events that were unavoidable.
31. Canovan, *Hannah Arendt*, 150.
32. Patricia Bowen-Moore, *Hannah Arendt's Philosophy of Natality* (New York: St Martin's Press, 1989) 122.
33. Bowen-Moore 123.
34. Lisa Jane Disch, *Hannah Arendt and the Limits of Philosophy* (Ithaca: Cornell University Press, 1994) 68.
35. Villa, *Politics, Philosophy, and Terror*, 190.
36. Young-Bruehl 324, 327.
37. Margaret Hull 69.
38. Elizabeth M. Meade, 'The Commodification of Values', in May and Kohn 117.
39. Richard J. Bernstein, 'Rethinking the Social and Political', *Hannah Arendt: Critical Assessments of Leading Political Philosophers*, ed. Garrath Williams (London: Routledge, 2006) III, 247–50 and Eli Zaretsky, 'Hannah Arendt and the Meaning of the Public/Private Distinction', *Hannah Arendt and the Meaning of Politics*, ed. Craig Calhoun and McGowan, John (Minneapolis: University of Minnesota Press, 1997) 225.
40. Hannah Fenichel Pitkin, *The Attack of the Blob: Hannah Arendt's Concept of the Social* (Chicago: University of Chicago Press, 1998) 4.
41. Hanna Fenichel Pitkin, 'Justice: On Relating Private and Public', in Williams III, 221.
42. Pitkin in Williams III, 223.

CHAPTER THREE
FREEDOM AND PRACTICAL POLITICS

1. *Men in Dark Times* will not be discussed in this chapter as it contains Arendt's views concerning various novelists and theorists that cohere with the rest of her political views, but involve more individual and idiosyncratic topics that do not broaden to a large degree the understanding of Arendt's overall political theory.
2. *On Revolution* has also been criticized for failing to describe the revolutions in both the United States and France accurately. E. J. Hobsbawn thinks that Arendt overgeneralizes and her theory fails to touch the historical phenomena of which she is concerned (E. J. Hobsbawn, 'Hannah Arendt on Revolution', in Williams II, 178). While he admits that Arendt's acute mind does have flashes of theoretical insight, her ideas do not adequately capture either revolution accurately. James Miller agrees that her method in *On Revolution* is baffling and her history is 'shoddy', claiming that Arendt's work is misleading about the American Constitution and about the French and Russian revolutions ('The Pathos of Novelty: Hannah Arendt's Image of Freedom in the Modern World', in Williams II, 182–3). Yet, Miller also asserts that Arendt's work provides a model for 'using the past to think about the possibilities of the present', so that its focus concerns the meaning of these events rather than the accuracy of them (Miller in Williams II, 198).
3. John F. Sitton, 'Hannah Arendt's Argument for Council Democracy', in Hinchman and Hinchman 311.
4. Sitton in Hinchman and Hinchman 311.
5. Sitton in Hinchman and Hinchman 309.
6. John McGowan, *Hannah Arendt: An Introduction* (Minneapolis: University of Minnesota Press, 1998) 157.
7. McGowan 157.
8. According to Arendt, Robespierre first sided with the small council bodies, but later went against them and placed power back in the assembly where it could be more easily controlled (*OR* 245–8).
9. Canovan, *Hannah Arendt*, 214.
10. Ronald Beiner, 'Rereading Hannah Arendt's Kant Lectures', in Williams IV, 262.
11. Arendt believes that the Declaration of Independence blurs the public and private sense of happiness, but at least the 'pursuit of happiness' in the Declaration is meant to include both aspects of happiness. In other words, happiness is not thought of as a strictly private phenomenon, but as a public one as well.
12. Leo J. Penta, 'Hannah Arendt: On Power', *The Journal of Speculative Philosophy* 10.3 (1996): 219.
13. Penta 220.
14. Iris Marion Young thinks that violence for humanitarian ends can be justified if the following conditions are met and if the UN or an international body sanctions the action: military force is the last resort, there is

good reason to believe it will be effective in attaining its humanitarian ends, it will be likely not to cause more harm than good, the military action will not undermine social infrastructure or cohesion of the country, and the consequences will be immediate, constrained and not destabilizing [Iris Marion Young, 'Violence against Power: Critical Thoughts on Military Intervention', *Ethics and Foreign Interventions*, ed. Deen K. Chatterjee and Don E. Scheid (Cambridge: Cambridge University Press, 2003) 262–5].

15. Miller in Williams II, 182.
16. Canovan, *Hannah Arendt*, 220–1.
17. Another key aspect for the successful foundation of the American government was the idea of the separation of powers. For the Americans, the division of powers among the branches of government allowed for the foundation of the Constitution and second, for the Supreme Court to continuously revise and interpret the Constitution (*OR* 201). Therefore, the foundation of the Constitution was not static, but could continuously adapt to new political circumstances through its interpretation by the Supreme Court. Bonnie Honig calls the kind of authority that comes from the Constitution as 'paradoxically enough, a practice of deauthorization', since it can be continually revised. It was a foundation that legitimized the rule of the people, but was flexible enough to admit and encourage questioning of its principles (Honig, 'Toward an Agonistic Feminism: Hannah Arendt and the Politics of Identity', in Williams II, 220).
18. Arendt also believes there could be a mixture of both conformism and juvenile delinquency in a child subjected to a lack of authority (*BPF* 182).
19. Honig in Williams II, 203.
20. Young-Bruehl 388, 421.
21. Young-Bruehl 421.
22. Young-Bruehl 421.
23. Arendt in Hill 333–4.
24. Arendt in Hill 334.
25. Arendt in Hill 334.
26. Arendt in Hill 309.
27. Agnes Heller, 'Hannah Arendt on Tradition and New Beginnings', *Hannah Arendt in Jerusalem*, ed. Steven E. Aschheim (Berkeley: University of California Press, 2001) 32.
28. Margaret Canovan, 'Hannah Arendt as a Conservative Thinker', in May and Kohn 14.
29. Young-Bruehl 417.
30. Young-Bruehl 418.
31. Young-Bruehl 391.
32. Young-Bruehl 390.
33. Young-Bruehl 391.
34. Young-Bruehl 416.

CHAPTER FOUR
THE LIFE OF THE MIND AND POLITICAL JUDGMENT

1. Arendt in Hill 305.
2. Arendt in Hill 338.
3. The withdrawal required for thought is not necessarily literal. Thinking can occur in the company of others, but there must be a mental withdrawal in order to hear one's own thoughts.
4. Arendt in Hill 303.
5. J. Glenn Gray, 'The Abyss of Freedom – and Hannah Arendt', in Hill 225.
6. Leah Bradshaw, *Acting and Thinking: The Political Thought of Hannah Arendt* (Toronto: University of Toronto Press, 1989) 85–6.
7. Bradshaw 88.
8. Gray in Hill 228.
9. Young-Bruehl xx.
10. It should be noted that Ronald Beiner and Maurizio Passerin d'Entrèves argue that Arendt has two models of judgment. The earlier model is meant to occur from the standpoint of the active life, and the later model supposedly occurs from the standpoint of the spectator, or the contemplative life, but this view is not agreed upon by all scholars and Arendt's thought will be presented in this chapter as one coherent position (Beiner in *KPP* 91, and d'Entrèves 103).
11. Immanuel Kant, *Critique of Judgment*, trans. Werner S. Pluhar (Indianapolis: Hackett Publishing Company, 1987) 18.
12. Kant 188–9.
13. The 'end' of action seems more complicated for Arendt than she openly articulates, since political actions can continue to reverberate long after they are thought to be completed. Therefore, the point at which judging begins is a bit vague, but since the judging process is revisable over time, it would be possible to revisit actions that continue to influence the community.
14. It should be noted that the faculty of taste is not literally attached to a specific sense-organ for Kant, and Arendt is changing and appropriating Kant's view for her own purposes on this point.
15. Kant 160; original emphasis.
16. Kant 161; original emphasis.
17. Alessandro Ferrara, 'Judgment, Identity, and Authenticity: A Reconstruction of Hannah Arendt's Interpretation of Kant', *Philosophy and Social Criticism* 24.2 (1998): 117.
18. Hannah Arendt Archives, McWherter Library, The University of Memphis, microfilm copy, 032415.
19. Ronald Beiner in *KPP* 108–9.
20. Bhikhu Parekh, *Hannah Arendt and the Search for a New Political Philosophy* (Atlantic Highlands, NJ: Humanities Press, 1981) 179.
21. Nancy Fraser, 'Communication, Transformation, and Consciousness-Raising', in Calhoun and McGowan 172.

CHAPTER FIVE
ARENDT'S CRITICS

1. McGowan 49.
2. Zaretsky in Calhoun and McGowan 225.
3. McGowan 76.
4. Richard J. Bernstein, 'Rethinking the Social and the Political', in Williams III, 248.
5. Bernstein in Williams III, 250.
6. Canovan, *The Political Thought of Hannah Arendt*, 105.
7. In addition, Canovan finds further ambivalence in Arendt's theory about the amount of power that humans have. Humans have a great deal of positive political power in free action, but also a large amount of negative, self destructive power in relation to the development of technology. At the same time, humans are somewhat powerless against of the forces of society and totalitarianism that manipulate humans beyond their control. Like the problem of the social, Arendt has also not explained how power and powerlessness work together (Canovan, *The Political Thought of Hannah Arendt*, 105–8).
8. Canovan, *Hannah Arendt*, 117–18.
9. Pitkin, *The Attack of the Blob*, 4, 16.
10. Pitkin, *The Attack of the Blob*, 16–17.
11. Pitkin, *The Attack of the Blob*, 16.
12. Pitkin, *The Attack of the Blob*, 199.
13. Pitkin, *The Attack of the Blob*, 199.
14. Pitkin, *The Attack of the Blob*, 250.
15. Arendt in Hill 317.
16. Arendt in Hill 317.
17. Arendt in Hill 318.
18. George Kateb, *Hannah Arendt: Politics, Conscience, Evil* (Totowa, NJ: Rowman and Allanheld, 1984) 28–42.
19. Kateb 35.
20. Seyla Benhabib thinks that the faculty of judgment can be thought as a moral faculty, in addition to a political one, despite Arendt's distinction between the two activities [Seyla Benhabib, 'Judgment and the Moral Foundations of Politics in Hannah Arendt's Thought', *Judgment, Imagination, and Politics: Themes from Kant and Arendt*, ed. Ronald Beiner and Jennifer Nedelsky (Lanham, MD: Rowman and Littlefield Publishers, Inc., 2001) 183–204].
21. Arendt in Hill 336.
22. Arendt makes this statement in reference to Dostoyevsky's *Possessed*.
23. Canovan, *The Political Thought of Hannah Arendt*, 124.
24. Arendt in Hill 326.
25. In 'Home to Roost', Arendt warns against the danger of escaping into utopias (*RJ* 275).
26. Hauke Brunkhorst, 'Equality and Elitism in Arendt', in Villa 178.
27. Brunkhorst in Villa 178.

28. In her later work that incorporates more of Arendt's archival material, Margaret Canovan finds Arendt's model of political action that is based upon the Greek antiquity to be complex and she believes that Arendt actually questions various aspects of Athenian democracy (Canovan, *Hannah Arendt*, 137–8).
29. Margaret Canovan, 'Politics as Culture: Hannah Arendt and the Public Realm', in Hinchman and Hinchman 199–200.
30. McGowan 66.
31. Hanna Fenichel Pitkin, 'Justice: On Relating Private and Public', in Williams III, 223.
32. For Arendt, councils are run by persons whose 'elitism' is derived from their self-selecting interest in politics.
33. Lewis P. Hinchman and Sandra K. Hinchman, 'In Heidegger's Shadow: Hannah Arendt's Phenomenological Humanism', in Williams IV, 18.
34. Arendt, Hannah. 'Heidegger at Eighty', *The New York Review* October 21 (1971) 51.
35. Arendt, 'Heidegger at Eighty', 53.
36. Arendt, 'Heidegger at Eighty', 53–4.
37. Bernstein 174.
38. Whitfield 194.
39. Whitfield 194.
40. Whitfield 194.
41. Elżbieta Ettinger, *Hannah Arendt/Martin Heidegger* (New Haven: Yale University Press, 1995) 10.
42. Wolin, Richard, *Heidegger's Children: Hannah Arendt, Karl Löwith, Hans Jonas, and Herbert Marcuse* (Princeton: Princeton University Press, 2001) 68.
43. Wolin 68.
44. Taminiaux ix.
45. Dana R. Villa, 'Totalitarianism, Modernity, and the Tradition', in Aschheim 326.
46. Villa in Aschheim 329.
47. Villa in Aschheim 335.
48. For Villa, Arendt seeks to show Heidegger as unpolitical or apathetic because of the unworldliness of his thought, rather than being anti-political (Villa, *Arendt and Heidegger*, 230).
49. Villa in Aschheim 337.
50. Jean Bethke Elshtain argues that children are immersed within political situations and therefore, cannot be spared from politics, making the separation of the social, political, and private far from distinct in Arendt's assessment of Little Rock [Jean Bethke Elshtain, 'Political Children', *Feminist Interpretations of Hannah Arendt*, ed. Bonnie Honig (University Park: Pennsylvania State University Press, 1995) 278].
51. Richard H. King, 'American Dilemmas, European Experiences', in Williams II, 231–2.
52. Ralph Ellison in Robert Penn Warren, *Who Speaks for the Negro?* (New York: Random House, 1965) 344.

53. Young-Bruehl 316.
54. Anne Norton, 'Heart of Darkness: Africa and African Americans in the Writings of Hannah Arendt', in Honig 259.
55. Norton in Honig 248, 256–7.
56. Joy James, 'All Power to the People!' *Race and Racism in Continental Philosophy*, ed. Robert Bernasconi with Sybol Cook (Bloomington: Indiana University Press, 2003) 250.
57. Robert Bernasconi, 'The Double Face of the Political and Social: Hannah Arendt and America's Racial Divisions', *Research in Phenomenology* 26 (1996): 12.
58. Richard H. King in Williams II, 228, 233.
59. Richard H. King in Williams II, 230.
60. Richard H. King in Williams II, 233.
61. Richard H. King in Williams II, 234.
62. Richard H. King in Williams II, 236.
63. Kristie M. McClure, 'The Odor of Judgment: Exemplarity, Propriety, and Politics in the Company of Hannah Arendt', in Williams IV, 292.
64. Elisabeth Young-Bruehl, 'Hannah Arendt among Feminists', in May and Kohn 307.
65. Hans Jonas, 'Acting, Knowing, Thinking: Gleanings from Hannah Arendt's Philosophical Work', *Social Research* 44 (1977): 26.
66. Young-Bruehl 272.
67. McGowan 35.
68. Mary G. Dietz, 'Feminist Receptions of Hannah Arendt', in Honig 20–3.
69. Adrienne Rich, *On Lies, Secrets and Silence* (New York: W.W. Norton and Company, 1979) 212.
70. Dietz in Honig 34.
71. Dietz in Honig 32.
72. Ann M. Lane, 'The Feminism of Hannah Arendt', in Williams II, 340.
73. Bat-Ami Bar On, 'Women in Dark Times: Rahel Varnhagen, Rosa Luxemburg, Hannah Arendt, and Me', in May and Kohn 300–1.
74. Young-Bruehl in May and Kohn 317–21.
75. Young-Bruehl in May and Kohn 322.
76. According to her niece, Edna Brocke, Arendt kept a low profile when she visited Israel during the Eichmann controversy (*JW* 514).
77. Feldman, Ron H., *The Jew as Pariah* (New York: Grove Press, 1978) 19.
78. Feldman 20.
79. Feldman 20.
80. Jennifer Ring, *The Political Consequences of Thinking: Gender and Judaism in the Work of Hannah Arendt* (Albany: State University of New York Press, 1997) 278.
81. Arendt in Hill 334.
82. Young-Bruehl 102.
83. Young-Bruehl 105.
84. Young-Bruehl 105.
85. Richard J. Bernstein, 'Hannah Arendt's Zionism?' in Aschheim 196.

86. Bernstein in Aschheim 198–9.
87. Bernstein 11.
88. Cristina Sánchez Muñoz, 'Hannah Arendt: Jerusalem or America? The Foundation of Political Community', in Williams II, 15.
89. Phillip Hansen, *Hannah Arendt: Politics, History, and Citizenship* (Stanford: Stanford University Press, 1993) 165.
90. Dagmar Barnouw, *Visible Spaces: Hannah Arendt and the German-Jewish Experience* (Baltimore: Johns Hopkins University Press, 1990) 241.
91. Barnouw 251.
92. Barnouw 251.
93. Bernstein 161.
94. Whitfield also notes that Arendt's forgiveness of Heidegger is in great contrast to her condemnation of the Jewish elders (195).
95. Whitfield 189, 191.
96. Gershom Scholem, '"Eichmann in Jerusalem": Exchange of Letters between Gershom Scholem and Hannah Arendt', in Feldman 242, 245.
97. Scholem in Feldman 241, 245.
98. Walter Z. Laqueur, 'Footnotes to the Holocaust', in Feldman 254.
99. Walter Z. Laqueur, 'A Reply to Hannah Arendt', in Feldman 278.
100. Hannah Arendt, '"Eichmann in Jerusalem": Exchange of Letters between Gershom Scholem and Hannah Arendt', in Feldman 249.
101. Arendt in Feldman 246.
102. Arendt in Feldman 247.
103. Young-Bruehl 339, 353.
104. Young-Bruehl 339.
105. Raymond Aron, 'The Essence of Totalitarianism according to Hannah Arendt', in Williams I, 146.
106. Whitfield 177.
107. Scholem in Feldman 242.
108. Walter Laqueur, 'The Arendt Cult: Hannah Arendt as Political Commentator', in Aschheim 61.

BIBLIOGRAPHY

MAJOR WORKS BY HANNAH ARENDT

Arendt, Hannah. *Between Past and Future: Six Exercises in Political Thought*. Cleveland, OH: Meridian Books, 1961.

—. *Crises of the Republic*. New York: Harcourt Brace Jovanovich, Inc., 1972.

—. *Eichmann in Jerusalem*. New York: Viking Press, 1963.

—. *Essays in Understanding 1930–1954: Formation, Exile, and Totalitarianism*. Ed. Jerome Kohn. New York: Schocken Books, 1994.

—. *The Human Condition*. Chicago: University of Chicago Press, 1958.

—. *The Jew as Pariah*. Ed. Ron H. Feldman. New York: Grove Press, Inc., 1978.

—. *The Jewish Writings*. Ed. Jerome Kohn and Ron H. Feldman. New York: Schocken Books, 2007.

—. *Lectures on Kant's Political Philosophy*. Ed. Ronald Beiner. Chicago: University of Chicago Press, 1982.

—. *The Life of the Mind*. Ed. Mary McCarthy. San Diego, CA: Harcourt Brace & Company, 1977.

—. *Love and Saint Augustine*. Ed. Joanna Vecchiarelli Scott and Judith Chelius Stark. Chicago: University of Chicago Press, 1996.

—. *Men in Dark Times*. New York: Harcourt, Brace and World, Inc., 1968.

—. *On Revolution*. New York: Viking Press, 1965.

—. *The Origins of Totalitarianism*. San Diego, CA: Harcourt Brace & Company, 1973.

—. *The Portable Arendt*. Ed. Peter Baehr. New York: Penguin Books, 2000.

—. *The Promise of Politics*. Ed. Jerome Kohn. New York: Schocken Books, 2005.

—. *Rahel Varnhagen: The Life of a Jewish Woman*. Trans. Richard Winston and Clara Winston. New York: Harcourt Brace Jovanovich, 1974.

—. *Reflections on Literature and Culture.* Ed. Susannah Young-ah Gottlieb. Stanford: Stanford University Press, 2007.

—. *Responsibility and Judgment*. Ed. Jerome Kohn. New York: Schocken Books, 2003.

Arendt, Hannah and Blücher, Heinrich. *Within Four Walls: The Correspondence between Hannah Arendt and Heinrich Blücher, 1936–1968*. Ed. Lotte Kohler. Trans. Peter Constantine. New York: Harcourt, Inc., 1996.

Arendt, Hannah and Heidegger, Martin. *Letters. 1925–1975: Hannah Arendt and Martin Heidegger*. Ed. Ursula Ludz. Trans. Andrew Shields. Orlando, FL: Harcourt, Inc., 2004.

Arendt, Hannah and Jaspers, Karl. *Hannah Arendt and Karl Jaspers Correspondence, 1926–1969*. Ed. Lotte Kohler and Hans Saner. Trans. Robert Kimber and Rita Kimber. San Diego, CA: Harcourt Brace & Company, 1992.

Arendt, Hannah and McCarthy, Mary. *Between Friends: The Correspondence of Hannah Arendt and Mary McCarthy, 1949–1975*. Ed. Carol Brightman. New York: Harcourt Brace & Company, 1995.

FOR FURTHER READING

Aschheim, Steven E., ed. *Hannah Arendt in Jerusalem*. Berkeley: University of California Press, 1999.

Beiner, Ronald and Nedelsky, Jennifer, eds. *Judgment, Imagination, and Politics: Themes from Kant and Arendt*. Lanham, MD: Rowman and Littlefield Publishers, Inc., 2001.

Benhabib, Seyla. *The Reluctant Modernism of Hannah Arendt*. Modernity and Political Thought Volume 10. Thousand Oaks, CA: Sage Publications, Inc., 1996.

Bernauer, James W., S.J., ed. *Amor Mundi: Explorations in the Faith and Thought of Hannah Arendt*. Boston College Studies in Philosophy Volume VII. Boston, MA: Martinus Nijhoff Publishers, 1987.

Bernstein, Richard J. *Hannah Arendt and the Jewish Question*. Cambridge, MA: MIT Press, 1996.

Bradshaw, Leah. *Acting and Thinking: The Political Thought of Hannah Arendt*. Toronto: University of Toronto Press, 1989.

Calhoun, Craig and McGowan, John, eds. *Hannah Arendt and the Meaning of Politics*. Minneapolis: University of Minnesota Press, 1997.

Canovan, Margaret. *Hannah Arendt: A Reinterpretation of Her Political Thought*. Cambridge: Cambridge University Press, 1992.

—. *The Political Thought of Hannah Arendt*. New York: Harcourt Brace Jovanovich, Inc., 1974.

Cavarero, Adriana. *For More Than One Voice: Toward a Philosophy of Vocal Expression*. Trans. Paul A. Kottman. Stanford: Stanford University Press, 2005.

D'Entrèves, Maurizio Passerin. *The Political Philosophy of Hannah Arendt*. London: Routledge, 1994.

Disch, Lisa Jane. *Hannah Arendt and the Limits of Philosophy*. Ithaca: Cornell University Press, 1994.

Hill, Melvyn A., ed. *Hannah Arendt: The Recovery of the Public World*. New York: St Martin's Press, 1979.

Hinchman, Lewis P. and Hinchman, Sandra K., eds. *Hannah Arendt: Critical Essays*. Albany: State University of New York Press, 1994.

Honig, Bonnie, ed. *Feminist Interpretations of Hannah Arendt*. University Park: Pennsylvania State University Press, 1995.

Kateb, George. *Hannah Arendt: Politics, Conscience, Evil.* Totowa, NJ: Roman & Allanheld, 1984.

May, Larry and Kohn, Jerome, eds. *Hannah Arendt: Twenty Years Later.* Cambridge, MA: MIT Press, 1996.

Pitkin, Hanna Fenichel. *The Attack of the Blob: Hannah Arendt's Concept of the Social.* Chicago: University of Chicago Press, 1998.

Ring, Jennifer. *The Political Consequences of Thinking: Gender and Judaism in the Work of Hannah Arendt.* Albany: State University of New York Press, 1997.

Taminiaux, Jacques. *The Thracian Maid and the Professional Thinker: Arendt and Heidegger.* Trans. and ed. Michael Gendre. Albany: State University of New York Press, 1997.

Villa, Dana. *Arendt and Heidegger: The Fate of the Political.* Princeton: Princeton University Press, 1996.

—. *Politics, Philosophy, Terror: Essays on the Thought of Hannah Arendt.* Princeton: Princeton University Press, 1999.

Villa, Dana, ed. *The Cambridge Companion to Hannah Arendt.* Cambridge: Cambridge University Press, 2000.

Williams, Garrath, ed. *Hannah Arendt: Critical Assessments of Leading Political Philosophers.* London: Routledge, 2006. Volumes I–IV.

Young-Bruehl, Elisabeth. *Hannah Arendt: For the Love of the World.* New Haven: Yale University Press, 1982.

—. *Why Arendt Matters.* New Haven: Yale University Press, 2006.

INDEX